M000314993

Crazy, Cracked, Warm, and Deep

Susan B. Clarke

Susan B. Clarke/Two Hummingbird Press
Contact Information: 704C 13th St. E. #124, Whitefish, MT
59927

Crazy, Cracked, Warm, and Deep/Susan B. Clarke. - 1st ed.

Paperback: 978-0-9994501-1-6
Hardcover: 978-0-9994501-4-7
Ebook: 978-0-9994501-3-0

Contents

Introduction

Crazy

Cracked

Warm

Deep

Foreword

It's easy to get caught up in Susan's story. It's powerful, compelling, righteous, and inspiring. That's incredibly attractive to over-achievers like me and all the C-suite executives Susan's coached over the last three decades. Getting it right, looking good, being right, these are all forms of winning. And for most of us, if we're honest, winning is a holy grail, a security blanket worth climbing mountains to get. It certainly has been for me, an Olympic rower, the only woman on an all-male Boeing flight test engineering team, an MBA grad striving to be "one of the boys" at Arthur Anderson, back in the day. And Susan's story of overcoming horrific childhood trauma and terminal cancer diagnoses (four times!) – talk about mountains climbed!

However, it would be a mistake to think this book is about winning – no. It's about living. The problem with "winning" is it requires an outward focus, a perfectionism, causing one to sacrifice one's inner connection in order to please others. Winning is so seductive, yet what many may fail to recognize, is it can be so deadening.

Instead, Susan is the master at living, at learning to become relational with ourselves, our stories, our loved ones, and our realities, rather than being right or perfect about any of it. It's messy, unscriptable, and demands a degree of surrender and vulnerability that makes climbing Mount Everest look like a cakewalk. It's a path she's taken over and over again, bringing her life.

All that aliveness shows up as passion, directness, intensity, and immediacy, which can be uncomfortable as hell to be around. There's nothing so enlivening as having an intense discussion with Susan and coming out the other side seen, heard, and changed. She'll tell you, in the moment, in front of anyone and everyone, if she thinks what you are saying is incongruent. This is not easy for a "look-good" person like me.

Susan cares deeply about helping people embrace, stand forward, and take responsibility for their own experience and life. While her fierceness may be intimidating to some, she's actually curious about you and your point of view. She is holding space for you to step forward into you, your mojo. You just have to be brave enough, in the face of her intensity, to keep engaging with her and being honest with yourself. When you do, she will meet you right there. It's what drove me to want to work with her, be around her, learn from her. It's her immediacy, her realness, her directness that consistently transforms leaders, business teams, couples, and anyone she coaches.

Susan has her own reasons for putting her writings together in this book that the rest of us get to read. For me, the gift in this book is that it is a physical manifestation of what being relational looks like. If Susan would let me anywhere near this text with my editor's pencil, I'd be all over this manuscript, editing, re-organizing, making "sense" out of it … based on my desire to make things look good. Thank god she's kept me out of it. This book definitely feels messy to me, unscripted even, in parts. And yet I come away with a felt sense of the magic and power in vulnerability and surrender … and a clear sense of how to practice this in my own life.

CrisMarie Campbell, MBA
Partner in love, life, and business

A Song From the Darkness

Words pouring onto the page

So innocent

Yet they flow with purpose

Painting a picture

The primary color black

But time and patience and the contrasting white becomes visible

More words, a war rages

Light and dark

Memories of pain and sorrow

A spark, a burning flame leaps onto the page

A flame so bright the eyes burn

Flesh burning

Then a Phoenix emerges

All captured in the simple words written on the page

The child sings, the woman stirs

The heart, the soul, and the song

Ring out

The picture comes to life

The life suddenly worth living

The scribe is born

The child's purpose becomes clear

So many years of silence

Never knowing how or why

But drawn to try

To find a way out of the silence

Not to revenge

Or fight back in anger or rage

But to create something other than darkness
The past becomes captured and transformed on the page
The story heard
Hidden in metaphor and prose
Only those of strength dare to question the reality
of the graphic pictures of murder and violence
All contained within a page
A simple combination of letters and words
Believe it if you like
Marvel at its creativity
Deny its possibility
Yet the picture remains on the page
& the eternal question
Could this happen to our children, to ourselves?
That question alone breaks the silence.

Introduction

Fractures and Fractals

What you need to know about me is I don't finish my sentences, and I don't finish my books. Well, that's not entirely true. I have co-written two books: *The Beauty of Conflict (for Teams)* and *The Beauty of Conflict for Couples* with my wife and business partner, CrisMarie Campbell.

What's more accurate is that I don't finish books that are focused on my personal story.

Now, if you are reading this, I finally did finish a book and a few sentences. But don't count on that being the case all the way through this book.

I am telling you about this right up front because I don't want to lose you with the first incomplete sentence or lead you to believe that this isn't a finished book.

It is.

Why don't I finish my sentences? Well, there are various reasons:

· I don't like finite conclusions or labels.
· I hate the end of a great story, book, TV series.
· I imagine I am supposed to be certain when I finish a sentence, and I'm rarely certain of anything.

Sentences, you see, are like people. You might imagine or believe that an unfinished sentence, thought, or story is bad, wrong, or broken.

An unfinished sentence is NOT broken, and frankly, I have yet to meet any broken people either!

So let me explain. This is a short digression into some of my philosophical underpinnings that might be helpful.

I want to talk about fractals and why they matter to me, and more importantly, this book.

Fractals are repeating patterns in nature. They can present looking like chaos, but behind that chaos is a pattern.

Fractals show up in nature all the time. Nature's examples include:

- Trees — the single trunk and the branches that emerge from it.
- Romanesco broccoli — a most stunning looking veggie, – plus tastes great!
- Patterns of streams, rivers, coastlines, mountains, waves, waterfalls, and water droplets — all fractals!

Remember studying geometry in school when you were figuring out how to create a right angle and various shapes and forms through equations and measurements? Yes, we build bridges and do so using these clear right-wrong formulas to ensure permanence and a solid structure. Out in nature nothing really shows up like that. Nothing in our natural world is held together by something that rigid, perfect, or permanent.

However, these fractals, these apparently chaotic patterns, somehow evolve into beauty and amazing aliveness in shape and form. Not rigid. Not permanent. Roots become a trunk which becomes branches and leaves.

We are part of nature and not perfect either, but we are also not broken or permanently fractured. We are fractals.

My life could so easily be seen as fractured.

I could say I was broken.

But I never liked geometry, though I was very good at math. I was horrible at geometry.

Those perfect right angles and precise measurements never made any sense to me.

I believe I was waiting for someone to introduce me to fractals.

These patterns that present like chaos but keep repeating in nature, offering an emerging, beautiful possibility with all the pieces somehow coming together to make a whole.

But let's be clear, that whole is also many, moving pieces. Beauty doesn't come from precision, perfection, or measured finished sentences.

At least my beauty doesn't, but I am beautiful, even with the unfinished sentences, gaps in my timelines, and emotional stories.

I don't want you to think this is going to be some book on all the ways that pain, heartache, and loss are just what I needed.

No. Many of my experiences sucked.

Though I would not trade them in, I wouldn't have complained about learning these lessons another way.

I did, though, have a strong desire to pull myself back together again, and thus *Crazy, Cracked, Warm, and Deep*, unfinished bits and all. Think fractal and read on.

Crazy

My Words Drip

Like blood splashed on paper
My words drip
Scars open and bleeding
Transformed in prose
There is always anxiety
A deep stirring inside my being
Reminding me that I am not asleep
Colors bright
Purple, green, black, and gold
Alive and pulsing
My being communicates through words
Written on a page
Flowing without thought or judgment
Sometimes sweet and sentimental
Sometimes filled with rage, blood red
Pouring out onto the page
My inner core is much different than my exterior
I try to bring more color to my page
But at times the fear prevails
I am left standing and silent
Only the prose to speak of the passion, the pain
I know that I am only able to live with the paradox on paper
So, I write, I write, I write
Reading only when my courage is great
Willing to learn of my parts
As though reading from a novel
Integrating when I am ready
Passing the words and the songs into life
To be sung, to be heard, to be honored

1.

Susie, Pull Yourself Back Together Again

Susie was out with her best friend picking daisies by the train track. The train hit Susie: thump. There's Susie scattered to pieces. Her friend calls out: "Susie, pull yourself back together again, it's time to go home." Susie did.

I remember and remember and remember that story over and over through the years. I also remember thinking: Thank goodness Susie could pull those pieces back together again and that she had such a good friend to remind her she needed to come home.

But pulling those pieces back together again was never quite as easy as the story makes it sound. Some pieces fit well and others I just jammed into place.

For the most part, I have learned how to come back home. But pieces of the puzzle still haunt me. Partially because those pieces never seem to fit, or even if they did, I wonder — "Is this really a piece of my puzzle?" Worse, someone else would ask, "Did that really happen?" or "Susie, you have such an imagination."

Over time, I came to some sort of peace that some of those haunting pieces that kept showing up were indeed mine, even if I didn't want to claim them.

One could say I finally accepted my crazy — not just accepted it, I became friends with it.

Imagine my surprise when I got an email from the past just a couple years ago.

Susie, I watched your TED Talk and wanted to connect. Don't know the best way to start but wanted you to know that while you were wrestling with cancer — I was facing my own past through homelessness.

I am about to have a book published and there are some pieces that I wanted you to know about.

One was already published but wasn't as directly revealing, this next one might be, and I wanted to tell you about it.

Then I read the published piece:

My older sister, Martha often shared this bedtime story. The plot went like this: Susie, my best friend and I were out picking daisies by the railroad track, Susie got hit by the train: thump. There was Susie all over the place in pieces. In the story I'd say, "Susie, pull yourself together again and come on home." Susie did.

My breath, stopped. My chest, tight. I could hardly inhale. Tears rolling down my cheek.

I thought it didn't matter anymore if someone out there said — "I remember too!" But it did.

That story was like the mantra for my childhood and

through the years of cancers and finding a way to piece the story back together.

Her message was like code that clicked the keys into place. Someone knew and had their own crazy in finding their path to being whole again.

I wasn't alone.

We did get together.

THE MEETING

My heart was racing. I scanned the little café. Only a handful of people.

Would I recognize her? Would she know me?

Gray hair and wrinkles for sure made me look different.

She must have some of the same.

Yes, there she was.

Her blue eyes were still as I remembered. She smiled. I could feel myself getting sucked back down the tunnel of time as I shifted my eyes to the knots in the wooden floor-boards.

"Hey," she said.

"Coffee? Tea?" I stuttered. Damn. I could feel my heart racing and the flutter in my gut.

"You need anything?" I worked to take a slightly deeper breath and exhale.

As I stood at the counter, I wrestled with the twitch in my legs compelling me to run.

I turned and walked slowly to the table.

She stood up and moved to greet me. Hug? Shake hands?

There was an awkward leaning and brushing of cheeks.

What do you do, meeting someone after 30-plus years? I had thought she was dead. She wasn't.

I didn't know how to start. She didn't either. I kept twirling my wedding ring waiting for an entry point.

> *Damn. Even now writing this I am stuck. Did we actually*
> *talk? What did we say? If we did talk about anything real,*
> *what could possibly have been the point of entry:*
> *What about that TEDx Talk made you call?*
> *Homelessness? Wow, I had no idea?*
> *By the way, do you remember the violent, bloody mess, like*
> *I do, from our early years?*
> *Did you think you were crazy forever?*

Surely, we didn't start there.

I can't remember.

Finally, she started. "I wrote another book. Not the one on homelessness, but more on my own trauma."

Her gaze shifted off into the distance. "I heard your screams, and I didn't do anything."

My eyes dropped. I took refuge again on a knot in the wood floor. My chest constricted.

"What could you have done?" I spoke.

"But I was hiding in the attic — I heard it all — I did nothing."

I looked up. She was still looking off in the distance.

"I don't think you could have done anything."

"He died horribly," she said. "I thought he got what he deserved."

"He was a horrible man." His blue eyes.

"I just wanted you to know." She looked right at me and said, "I knew and I'm sorry I didn't do more."

I felt foggy and numb.

"I moved here. Far, far away and that helped. I couldn't … reach out."

"I'm glad he's gone," I said, long exhale.

I couldn't raise my eyes or even move my arms off the table.

"You have a son, right?" I was trying to remember any bits of information I had gathered online. "You moved here after the homelessness? You got a theology degree too, right?"

"Yes — I walked out — left my husband, my home." She brushes some crumbs from the table. "My son and I are closer now."

Oddly, I know what she means. Like me with my sisters.

"I enjoy teaching," she continues.

"They told me you committed suicide. I thought you were dead."

For a flash her eyes harden and seem cold. I felt my chest tighten.

Then her eyes soften.

"My family would never say I was on the streets and homeless. I didn't know that was the message. But it doesn't really surprise me. I felt dead."

The tear rolling down my cheek caught me by surprise.

You'd be better off dead. Words I had heard myself.

"I'm glad you're not dead."

"So am I. Now."

I glance and notice the café is now full.

Time to go.

We hug.

I leave.

THE PHONE CALL BACK HOME

Later, on the phone with CrisMarie —

"I did it. It felt so confirming." My words, fast and light.

"What did she say?" CrisMarie wanted the details.

"Some things about her life and that she did hear the screaming. He died horribly." I burst out.

"Susan, that's it? That was the conversation?" Her tone annoyed or maybe perplexed.

"Well, yeah." The lightness gone from my words.

"Did you talk about the puppies?" she asked. "The other memories?"

"Well — no. I didn't need to." My eyes focused on the carpet.

"Okay, I get your struggle. But I thought she wanted to talk."

"We did." *Didn't we?*

"I am not trying to be mean or judge, but it sounds like a lot of pieces were missing." Her voice, softer and concerned. She continued. "Like, was the screaming the incident when you were raped and hospitalized? Did you talk about that?"

"Well of course the screaming was when I was raped." I squeezed the phone and got louder.

"Did you ask?' she said, measured and slow.

"No — of course not." A long sigh. Shoulders slump.

"What about the puppies?" *The puppies.*

"No — look, I knew she knew." *The puppies — why does she have to bring up the puppies? Who would talk about that?* My body now tight and tense.

"Sorry, really, I'm not trying to make you wrong. But I know you've never talked to anyone from back then who shared your story." I could feel the gentleness through the line.

Tears rolled down my cheeks, my chest pounding.

"I know, I know, and I did my best."

"I get it."

I really hadn't said much. Still, the pieces did fit into place. Didn't they?

BACK TO THE BOOK

Fractals.

I still love picking daisies, and as a result have been whacked by a few trains — only to have the pieces scatter again.

It's amazing what can be created between the words. Maybe more "real" than the story itself — the heartbeats and felt sense of being on the right path.

2.

Silent Yet Screaming Inside

There's this knot that aches in my chest.

It goes away when I see my dog play at the dog park or listen to a piece of music, but it doesn't take long to come back.

When I turn inward, that knot belongs to a little girl inside. I promised her I'd take some time to write. To see if words, or telling her stories, would help heal or at least allow the grief to flow.

There is so much about my life now that I love! I love my relationship. I love our dogs, Rosie and ZuZu, who think life is all about play. I love living in Montana.

It's true, lots of my life is good! Very good. So where does the deep ache come from?

Maybe it's hard to be happy when I see so many people suffering. There is so much that goes on inside as I watch the news, read about the shootings of black men and of white policemen, listening as people around me talk about racism, sexism, homophobia, politics, being white, being black, being young, being old, just being human. I often stay silent. But I am not quiet inside.

Maybe it is about how all lives should matter, not just white ones, and how some people have to work harder to get that point across.

The thing is, I am part of all this. I am racist, sexist,

homophobic. I probably don't know the half of it. The events of my life color how I put my world together, and I make judgments in a heartbeat. Sometimes I'm conscious of it, sometimes not. I believe it's how we humans are wired. It is the best of us and the worst of us.

And so, I can certainly educate myself about cultural diversity and learn about the history of systemic white privilege, and I am. It's important to know. But unless I also pay attention to the very personal and emotional filter of my life, it's not going to make much difference.

And so, when I hear that little girl screaming inside, I must pay attention.

She asked me to tell her story, to write my book, and I keep getting stuck.

Stuck living in this moment or that next one, and the book goes into the background.

Until a day like today, when she feels so angry because she hears that she was privileged.

My little girl doesn't get it.

I tell my little girl there's truth to that — that white privilege is real and that my life really could have been worse.

She does not agree.

It's not that simple.

She remembers how it felt when she was raped at four (and again over and over). She remembers how it felt when she spoke up about his horrible acts and was called imaginative.

She remembers the much-loved, charismatic camp director who preached goodness and for years chose to do whatever he damn well pleased after dark.

She knew. She tried to tell. No one listened.

She screams, "It's not fair!"

It isn't.

He wanted her silenced.

She got angry and punched a hole in the wall.

The doctor said she had an anger problem and gave her drugs.

Life moved on.

There was school and the dyslexic issue. But being laughed at for misspellings and not being able to read — that was nothing. You know — sticks and stones and rape and broken bones — that at least had passed — words would really never hurt her.

Except they did.

Then there was fifth grade, where she was at a predominately black school.

There was Charlotte.

Charlotte bullied her regularly.

She spoke up. No one did anything.

She ran for student council president based on the platform to stop bullying.

She got one vote — hers, which got broadcast over the public speakers in homeroom.

She wanted to cry and ran to the bathroom.

Charlotte was in the bathroom.

Tears were not going to help.

She moved on and found a path playing tennis, hockey, and basketball. She had loved Little League, but you know — girls older than nine couldn't play baseball — even if they were much better than the boys.

She was fortunate to be athletic. Baseball may be out, but there were other games to play and ways to run, run, and run from feeling the ache beneath her white skin.

Ugly and athletic. That worked once she hit high school and was the only white girl in an inner-city black school. Sure, there are some downsides. Like when the TV series *Roots* played for two weeks. She hated being white. What white person wouldn't, seeing the atrocities committed against black people? Yet, as the poster white kid, she got thrown against lockers, jeered at, and beaten up each day during those two weeks for being white.

She was a survivor, creative, and resilient.

Of course, when being white might have finally been a benefit, heading to college at the University of Virginia, by this time she was, I'll just say, different.

She tried to fit in, and she did some things really well.

When she arrived, she came with a hammock and her mummy sleeping bag, intending to sleep out on the porch. Her roommate snapped some pictures of the setup and had a few girls in the hall laughing about the "outdoor" girl. The hammock came down and the mummy bag hung in the closet, used only for weekend runs to the woods.

She regularly saw most people in Polo shirts and khakis. She invested in a few new Polo knockoffs. Needless to say, the girls in her hall quickly let her know the knockoffs had the polo stick on the wrong side. Another chuckle. She dumped the Polo shirts for a few rugby shirts — orange and blue, UVA colors, and that seemed to work.

She soon learned that her best bet was to stay far away from the dorms and mostly hang out with the other athletes.

Well, until some upperclasswomen started to come on to her in the bathroom, and she freaked out. The only solution was to move into a house with all guys. The guys thought she was a lesbian (basketball and sports) and her teammates thought she was with one of the guys in her house. She never said a word.

However, there was a cost...

There was a lot about life that just kept hammering away at her creative spirit.

After a number of years fighting cancer in her twenties, she did find a home, a place that welcomed her and made it okay for her to be different. She started learning to be self-responsible and relational.

Not that being self-responsible and relational were easy. Taking responsibility for her life was hard, lonely, hellish at times. But she found her way and finally found a way to integrate — not get rid of — her past.

She found her loving. She didn't think that it much mattered that it was with a woman. And it really didn't, but that doesn't mean it wasn't one more thing that made her different.

So back to me today and the ache in my chest. Yes, on the outside I stand looking white, gray-haired, and privileged. I get it. I am that white woman who made it out of my past.

3.

Why I Write

When I was seven, I was gifted a live baby rabbit that had been saved from the camp lawn mower. I was thrilled to take the little being in my hands. Feel its rapid heartbeat. I found the bunny a home in a box, which I made quite comfy with grasses, leaves, and dirt. I was so ready to protect and nurture the little being. I sat beside that box for hours watching it breathe and feeling its heartbeat.

Late in the day, my mom called me to go to dinner. We had to leave our cabin for the lodge. I would be gone for at least an hour or more. I knew I needed to protect the bunny from our dog and the camp cat, so I put the box in our car. Off I went to dinner. When I returned, I found the baby rabbit very still, clearly not breathing — dead. The car had gotten too hot. I was devastated. I couldn't find words for what I was feeling. The horror that *I* had killed the little baby bunny was overwhelming. I didn't speak about it. I went quiet for days. I silently buried the rabbit. I didn't know how to come back.

When I returned to school, my teacher asked us all to write about our summer. On that blank sheet of paper, I reclaimed my heart. I wrote about the joy I felt with a new life in my care. The pleasure of creating a home. The hours of being a protector. The tragic choice to put the little bunny in the car. A decision made with good intent that went horribly wrong. Finally, the pain of holding that little lifeless bunny. The piece wasn't long. It was a series of simple words with some missing and some misspelled. Yet those words captured the life and death of my bunny. When my teacher chose that piece to read and I heard my words, I finally cried. My life returned. The pain was freed to live forward.

Since that first piece, I have used writing as a path to process the stories of my life that otherwise would have shut me down.

When I write, my heart opens. My defenses drop and the armor I've used to survive begins to melt.

When I was dealing with cancer, I wrote to wrestle with the gods about fairness. When I was dealing with nightmares and memories, I used prose to share the pain that was trapped in my cells. When I am holding a space in a circle for peoples' stories that are not mine to share, I write to find my heart, clear my mind, so that I can stay present and connect with their world, not stay stuck in mine.

Writing frees my emotions and clears my pain so that the dark spots get the needed light to live forward. Writing allows the broken pieces to reform and become art.

I have wrestled with creating a book that tells a complete story from beginning to middle to end. Instead, my path seems to be more an ongoing river of short pieces that repeat patterns, fractals.

I never called myself a writer because my written words were rarely kept. I'd share them in circles and with friends. In the sharing, my armor would finally soften. That still seems to be the heart of my purpose in writing.

I know I am a better person when I write. My defenses

drop and my heart opens when I let the words find a place on a page. The cracks those words create let the light in and my broken heart beats on.

The memory of a baby bunny's journey in my hands is complete — life and death, joy and sorrow.

No hero.

No happy-ever-after ending.

Real, raw, and messy.

Human after all.

4.

I Want Botox

"I want Botox!!" the little girl is screaming.

Deep inside, I do too. I totally get her desire to take away the ugly scars, wrinkles, and angry lines: traces of a face that was designed to keep everyone away.

Whenever the world presents me with uncertainty and I'm forced to wrestle with intense thoughts or feelings, my face hardens. Deep ridges have formed between my eyebrows from all that frowning. There are grooves etched around eyes that readily narrow into slits. My mouth now naturally curves downward even when I'm relaxed; people are always wondering if I'm angry or upset.

The muscles don't readily lift into a smile unless I laugh — which apparently changes everything. My color returns, my eyes twinkle, and I have a dimple that naturally comes out. But most of the time my face is an unreadable mask, often interpreted as angry or intense. "Opaque," someone once called it: hard to understand and impenetrable.

My face reflects the ongoing work of living with my choices. I picked a life that protected me from remembering things that were too painful. But no matter how much work I've done from the inside out, the reflection in the mirror still shows the strategy of one who doesn't want to be touched, the leftover lines of someone trying desperately to be tough, strong, and distant. Oh, how I sometimes wish

I could be Barbie. Beautiful, flawless, with a face that shows no trace of a life hard lived.

Brené Brown is my hero. I listened to her TED Talk about vulnerability; she gave me the language to understand myself. But then I saw her being interviewed by Oprah. She looked more like a model than a researcher. I doubt I'm being fair to Brené Brown. It's just that she looked so happy, relaxed, and at ease. Could the person behind that beautiful face really understand what I've been through? My heart aches.

"I want Botox!!"

No wonder that little girl screams for Botox or a facelift. Something that would erase the wrinkles on my face. Something that would let the world know that the past is simply part of a rich landscape, not who she is now. Something so that people would no longer see the crazy, angry one who isn't soft. Because the caring that is so vast inside isn't obvious to the world outside and that still stabs at my heart sometimes.

Of course, the people who see my face don't know my stories. How I was raped by the beloved camp director when I was four, the man who told the authorities, "Best not to listen to her wild story. She has quite an imagination, that little girl." How he sealed my silence by killing a litter of puppies in front of me, telling me it was my fault because I'd threatened to expose him. Unable to speak of my pain, I punched a hole in the wall when I got home and was ordered to a doctor for my anger issues. He gave me drugs that numbed everything but did nothing to stop the violation and pain inside me.

I survived by keeping people away. I took on many personas so no one would know what I cared about because then they could hurt me.

I was masterful at hiding, until I got cancer. Suddenly, my body was a mess of scars and contradictions that forced me to stop lying and remember. The cancer was going to be my way out; instead, it was my path in.

Many times, I was only willing to talk about my painful past because I was planning on dying. But then another wrinkle: I survived. I was stuck living with the nightmares and the stories. Oh, to be able to take a pill or surgically recover that youth and innocence I gave up just to stay alive. It would be great if it were that easy!

"I want Botox," the little girl screams once more.

I simply sit next to her. Waiting for the wailing to stop. I can wait. I am here. No Botox. No surgery. Here with all the lines and wrinkles of the past. Here now, finally. I'm ready to tell her story. My story.

5.

When a Fight is Right

I was one of only two white kids in my high school. Everyone else was black. Not a mix of Asian, Latin, Mexican, or a diverse grouping of nationalities. No, aside from one boy, David, and myself, everyone else referred to themselves as black. Now, you may be thinking I am saying that because it was a problem. No, that is not the story here. As a matter of fact, being the only white female helped me fit in. Anything odd about me I simply attributed to being white. Here are a couple of examples.

Most of my teammates at school dated or at least shared stories of boys. Not me. There was one time when Stephanie asked, "Hey, white girl! What's with you? Don't white girls date?"

I was silent.

Then Wendy laughed and said, "Who are you kidding? White girls don't date, they wait, right?"

I'd stayed silent then slowly nodded. Why not? If it silenced the storm, sure, white girls wait.

Then, in the girls' locker room, Tonia, a teammate, reached across and rubbed her hand on my leg.

"What — no hair?" she asked. "Wow, is that a white girl thing too?"

Again, I just didn't answer. I'd never had any hair on my arms or legs, but since that seemed odd, why should I have it define just me. I just let it define all white girls.

When it came to makeup, I never touched it — still don't. However, makeup was fairly common with my teammates.

"What's with you — no makeup? You know that skin could use some color." The usual banter as most of the team was gathered around the mirror applying various skin products.

"Another white girl thing?" Spoken with a pause.

Me. Silence. Why comment?

Truthfully, both my older sisters had been wearing makeup for years, probably since they were 12. Both dated. Both shaved. There had been boys coming to the house for one of them from a young age. No. I just was a bit different.

Anyway, I liked being able to let folks assume anything different was simply a cultural piece. This worked for me.

The reason I asked to stay in the public schools even when it was clear I was going to be in a significant minority was because I loved sports and wanted the best athletic program. In my mind, there was no question that was at John Marshall High School. I was determined to play every sport possible. I arrived as a great tennis player. Now, that was a sport where John Marshall needed some strong players if they were going to have a chance. I had a natural spot to fit in.

But really, I wanted to play basketball. If you could see me, you would wonder why. I am not tall, nor am I gifted in jumping or really shooting for that matter. But I wanted to play on a team, and I knew that was the best team at the school. I was determined to try out.

Well, the way it worked was, since basketball was a popular sport, the coach held a two-week tryout period. Anyone could show up and each practice lasted two to four hours. The first half of any practice was conditioning, and we did that with the guys. Eighty girls tried out. Maybe it was 50 — but it seemed like 80. Honestly, I cannot be certain about the numbers. The workouts were HARD. But one thing I am very good at is surviving, and I can hang in through most anything.

Part of why the practice was so hard in the conditioning realm was to weed out the faint of heart. Lots of the girls dropped after the first week. By week two, there were 40 of us. The biggest issue for me was that in every game situation I would be punched or slapped. We are not simply talking rough basketball — but white-girl-must-go pop shots.

I was determined not to cave. Week two got worse. However, I convinced the coach to keep working with me because I was one of the only girls who was not interested in shooting. I loved passing the ball, and I could tell he needed someone who wasn't only interested in scoring. The problem for me was dealing with the constant rough stuff — pushing, hitting, elbowing. After two weeks, I figured I might get cut, but I wasn't going to quit or complain.

The day the coach called out the 15 of us who would be making the team I was the second to the last name called. Stephanie, a 6'2" freshman, was after me. Being 6'2" was the gift for her but she had yet to catch a ball — we both knew we were not picked for our basketball skills.

The next couple weeks were constant drills and team set-ups. It was clear some of the regular girls did not like that the white girl made the team. During practice, any time the coach's back was turned, I'd get kicked or tripped. In the locker room, more than once I would get slammed from behind. I went home most days in tears. Still, I did not want to quit.

Finally, we were starting to play games. I was a second team point guard. We were playing the first string and getting whopped. But I was playing some good defense. I was man-to-man on the best senior player, Sonja, and I'd managed to keep her from scoring. She was on fire. She was coming down the court with the ball; I was clearly set in her path. She did not slow down a step. She came right at me and knocked me hard to the floor. As I was getting up, she pushed me right back down. I waited for a whistle. Nothing. I started to get up again, and she just sat on me. Something happened in that moment, and I suddenly rolled her off me. I stood up and turned to her.

"Okay, you want a fight, let's fight." I had my fist up. I have never hit a person. I did once put a hole in the wall, but I had no idea how to fight a person. Still, I was furious.

She looked at me. Her eyes like lasers and her jaw tight and incredibly hard — looking through me. I braced myself for her fist. But all that came was the stare. Maybe it was a second or maybe it was 10 minutes. Time was still.

"Well, it's about time." The stare was suddenly a slight smile.

"You are finally willing to defend yourself. Damn, girl, you need to work on that shit. No way should you ever have to put up with the shit we've been dealing you."

I was stunned. My fist still up and ready if needed. I was shaking. I finally looked around. Every person in the gym was watching. Even the guys were gathered. I had no idea.

"You are okay — maybe we were wrong to push, but hell, you weren't on this team for your scoring skills — and we didn't just want you because you were white. You gonna speak?"

I dropped my fist. "Really? This was a test?!"

"Well, no — not everyone gets the crap you've been getting. I got to admit I didn't want a white girl on the team. I was ready to do whatever it took to get you to quit. But damn, girl, you are determined. Now I got to like you."

Wow! I wasn't really sure I was ready to call her a friend.

"You don't have to like me, but just stop with all the whacking and pushing."

Oddly, Sonja became my best friend by the end of the season. Getting on the team was the hardest part, but I was the only white basketball player in my district. So often I was hassled in other gyms or out on the courts. Sonja would not let a thing get by her and no one liked to mess with Sonja, so life did get easier.

At least until...

What I failed to mention was that previously John Marshall was the state champion and had been for a few years. We were the team to beat. Now, I had made the team, but most of my playing time was subbing in for Wendy, the best point guard I've ever watched, or coming in late in the half or once a game was out of reach. So yes, I got lots of name-calling and such but wasn't on the court for too long. Plus, I had Sonja.

There was the day we played our biggest rival in their very small gym. The bleachers were limited, and fans stood right on the sidelines, surrounding the court. The gym was packed. We knew this would be our toughest game. Wendy started the game, but very quickly got into foul trouble.

"Susie? You're in."

I stood and pulled off my sweats and headed to the table to check in.

"Honky, Honky!!" In the small-packed space, it seemed very intimidating.

As the referee signaled me in, there was a loud hissing sound from the crowd. Wendy gave me a high five. "Don't let it get to you," she mouthed as she passed by.

I quickly moved to defend and within a second got my hand on the ball. I was trying to control the steal and very close to the sideline. A leg came out from the crowd, and I fell on my face. No whistle. The crowd laughed and cheered.

I got up. Sonja's voice came from somewhere, "You okay, girl?"

"Yes" was spoken from somewhere inside me. The game was very fast, aggressive, and loud. Whenever I touched the ball, the crowd hissed, yelling "HONKY!" If I got close to the sidelines, I got yelled at, pushed, or tripped.

At my best, I'm not Wendy, and on this day, I was not even close to good enough to keep us in the game. Wendy came back in but fouled out. As I entered with 8 minutes still on the clock, I knew we were in big trouble.

The crowd got more wound up as the clock wound down, and I stayed on the court. The bleachers were vibrating, feet stomping. The energy in the gym was escalating into a frenzy.

Suddenly, the doors to the gym flew open and in walked eight armed police officers. They headed to our coach and had a brief chat. A timeout was called, and the coach motioned me over to him.

"They are here to take you out of the gym. They are concerned about a riot if you stay and 'specially your safety."

"Well, it isn't like I'm helping a lot here."

Both Wendy and Sonja spoke up at the same time. "No way she goes alone. If she walks, we walk."

"We'll forfeit if that happens and lose our undefeated record, possibly a spot in state," the coach said.

"If she goes, we go."

I was silent. Who would have ever thought, after the way we started, things would end up like this?

The entire team circled me. The police made a circle around them. As we exited from the gym and the forfeit was announced, there was a rush toward us. Sonja took my hand. No way was anyone getting to me without going through her.

Indeed, we lost that day and didn't get the call to state. However, Sonja and Wendy, both seniors, said that was one of their high points, walking off that court with me.

Sonja: "The game isn't always about who's ahead when the buzzer sounds. Walking out with you that day, I was proud. Never forget — you are alright — even if you are white!!"

I went on to play basketball throughout high school. Always the only white kid in the district, but it was never as rough as those first few weeks. Sure, I had lots of angry people when we played at other schools, but I could always hear Sonja's voice, "Don't let 'em get to you. You may be white, but you are alright."

6.

Surprising Yale

As for basketball, I stuck with it. I played each year. Our first year we were great. After our senior stars left, we really struggled. At one point, we were 1-15, which was the worst record in the history of John Marshall's women's team.

Coach Threats kept saying, "You guys suck right now, but sometimes losing is the only path to eventual greatness — don't quit!"

In my senior year, we'd become more like the champion teams of the past. Well, maybe not undefeated but pretty damn good.

Imagine my surprise when Coach Threats pulled me aside one day after practice.

"Susie, I got a call today from Yale. They want to come down for a recruiting visit."

Wow! Yale — now that was a damn good school. I admit I was having a little trouble wrapping my mind around how this was a reality.

Don't get me wrong — I am not dumb — I did well on my SATs in math and science but not great on verbal.

"Look — here's the deal — I am pretty sure Yale thinks you are black."

Okay — now if that was true, well, maybe I understood. This was a period where schools were looking to bring in minorities.

"Why would they assume that?" I said without much thought.

"Well — we have one other white student. Our district is almost all black. You play basketball and are the top of your class. I don't think they ever assumed you could possibly be white."

Threats was smiling.

"I would never want to put you in a bad spot, but I would love to see their faces should we say yes, and they see your white-self come walking in." Threats was almost laughing! (He hardly ever laughed!)

I took a moment to think about my answer. Yale was NOT a school I had any interest in attending. I loved my coach and had nothing but respect for both him and our athletic director Christian, who was equally happy about this possible moment.

I was game. "Go for it — let's bring them down here!"

They made it happen.

The day Yale was scheduled to come for the visit, I had agreed to let Threats, Christian, the athletic director, and my principal, take the lead. I would join them as the day went on.

Imagine my surprise when I heard that there were three white men and a white woman walking the halls with Threats and Christian, getting the rundown on our athletic department.

I was a touch nervous. I was not being recruited by any other schools — not for basketball. Yes, there were some schools that were interested in me as a tennis player and a couple even for an Engineering scholarship — but no one

47

was knocking hard at the door — much less sending a team of people.

I got called to the office mid-day. As I walked down the hall, I was nervous. I also had a moment of thinking this was pretty cool — maybe they were interested. Mostly, I was doing this for my coach. Maybe a small part of me wanted to believe this could happen, could be about me.

I had to sit outside the principal's office for a few minutes waiting to get the call.

As I walked in — I watched the faces of all four Yale representatives show signs of disbelief and stunned surprise. I walked right up and boldly spoke.

"Hi — I am Susie Clarke — I am thrilled you guys are interested in me!" I reached my hand out to each of them.

We did shake hands, but those hands all seemed a bit limp to me and not many words came out of their mouths! They were silenced.

The smiles I caught on the faces of Threats and Christian were priceless.

I sat.

There was an awkward period of silence.

"Look — ahh — I think we are indeed impressed with the stats we have on you." Finally, one of the Yale representatives spoke.

"We really wanted to come see you — and get a feel for your interest. There is no guarantee..." The string of words had a few gaps.

"You thought I was black, didn't you?" I just decided to say the obvious.

"Well — we did think you were a minority student."

"Well I am — I am only one of two white students here at John Marshall and have been in the minority for years now."

"Well — " another long pause

"Look, we assumed you were Afro-American. At Yale, you would not be a minority and this particular scholarship is for minorities."

"I thought it was for basketball, and trust me, in basketball I am a real minority!!!"

I wasn't going to let them off easy. I could almost feel the joy and satisfaction coming off of Threats and Christian.

I don't think they often got the chance to make a room full of white people go speechless.

I don't remember word-for-word the rest of the interview. It ended with an invitation for me to apply as a regular student.

I never heard from Yale again.

Later, Threats and Christian called me to their office.

They were laughing out loud, which was rare.

"Look, Susie — I know that must not have been easy — but I loved watching their faces. I do hope you're okay. They really are missing out on a damn good student and point guard — even if you are white."

We all laughed.

I have no regrets about that experience.

These days, I've shared the story and people have encouraged me to go back and sue Yale.

Really?

I think I had made the impact I wanted to make.

I am pretty sure Yale started checking closely — more than just test scores, stats, and district racial percentages.

People are always more than stats and — even though I get I wasn't a "minority" — I was definitely playing against the odds.

YEARS LATER

People ask me to tell this story. It can be funny. Some get very angry about it and others think I am trying to back away from owning my white privilege.

The story wasn't, or isn't, about me. I loved that my coach, my athletic director, and my principal — all black men who had been dealing with the recruiting and the system forever — asked me if I would play along.

They said it was one time where they felt some sense of "power."

They know too often players are just diversity numbers and that universities aren't really interested in the overall well-being of the athlete. They just need to fill a quota. That conversation has happened too many times, and for once they wanted to watch the white man (or woman) be the one uncomfortable.

I agreed.

When I went on to the University of Virginia, one of my best friends joined me. She was a black woman. I saw how she was treated. It was like she didn't exist. She was a stat. When we'd leave practice or a class we had together, I'd get invited to come join an activity and nothing for her. I'd invite her and soon neither of us were invited.

I was horrified. You don't just ignore people. I fully understood why she was pissed. She had every reason to be angry, and yet it was as though she didn't even exist. She transferred to another school where she shined. No one deserves to not exist.

I know in my years at John Marshall I did get beaten up a lot because I was white. That was uncomfortable. However, I did know that I existed.

That day with Yale, I sat there and felt for only a few moments that I, the person, did not exist. They were only looking for someone with black skin. I can't really imagine how hard that would be to live with over an entire lifetime.

Cracked

To Love and Hate

Is it best to say I love you — when sometimes I wish you
were dead?
Is it okay to say I love you — when there are things about
you I don't even like?
Is it wise to send you letters — when I never want you
to reply?

Tell me please
Someone please tell me

Is it possible to feel such a range of feelings for one person
To remember horrors and kindness
Kindness and horrors
To flip so freely from light to dark
Is it possible to believe me and you
And not be hypocritical?

Tell me please
Someone please tell me

I call out these questions as though someone knows
How, I ask myself, could this not be so

I do love you and sometimes wish you were dead
I do love you and know there are many things about you I
do not like
I have written to you and I do not want you to write back

It is best that I do these things
Best because I could never say I love you if the other could
not be included.

It must be possible simply because it is so
There was kindness and horrors
And I do believe me and you
So I guess I need not ask anymore
I know

At least I am not indifferent

7.

Velcro Shoes

Being the youngest of three girls, I grew up at the mercy of my older sisters' teasing. I was somewhat of an odd duck in the trio, in that both of my sisters were brilliant and smart. I would never have used those words for myself. I was dyslexic, and aside from the horrible spelling and reading problems, the other way my dyslexia showed up was the way I tied my shoelaces — apparently, backwards.

"Hey Susie, — come over here and join in the fun."

Of course, I would head over with joy at getting a chance to play with the big kids.

"How about Simon Says?"

"I know that one." I was thrilled.

Penny, my oldest sister, is Simon. The rest of the girls and I lined up facing her.

"Simon Says — jump ten times."

Easy!! We are all successful.

"Simon Says — tie your shoes."

I am all over that. Just after untying my shoes, I start to re-tie them, I hear the laughter.

"See — backwards!!" Everyone is laughing. No one is tying their shoes but me, and obviously, there's something odd about how I am doing it. I am hot, flushed, and hurt.

"Is not — don't ..." But I give up. There's no point. The laughter is loud. I can tell my words are just making the laughter worse. I run off.

Mumbling under my breath, "I tie my shoes," I stop and start tying my shoes again. And again. A tear rolls down my cheek. "Good enough." More of a knot than a bow.

As a result of my stubborn nature, I refused to believe there was a damn thing wrong with how I tied my shoes. No. I didn't want to be different. Yet, I was already labeled different. I couldn't read and struggled with spelling.

To cope, I got my sister to read my school books out loud to me at night. I had learned to recall word for word what she read. The next day, when I asked to read out loud, I could recite the section. I thought that was pretty cool — different but cool.

I had arranged a deal with Andy, the best speller in my class. I picked him for my kickball team at recess, and he let me copy his spelling test. I never did it perfectly, just well enough to get by. Until I got caught. That resulted in almost a year of after-school remedial class. I had enough teasing about that. I was good with how I tied my shoes.

I kept tying them "backwards" right through college.

Sure, over the years, as a high school and college basketball player, my shoe tying created some laughs for my teammates, but I was a good enough athlete that most people thought the way I tied my laces was some sort of psychological edge. I never said a word, I just kept tying them backwards and never let the laughter sink in.

In my twenties, life offered me one of the toughest challenges: cancer. It didn't start out that way. Hell, I was 23 and full of vim and vigor. I'd finally landed in a job I loved, working with kids, teaching, and coaching. I was happy, though in hindsight, I was still very different.

I'd never been in any significant relationship. I had friends; as soon as anyone got too close, I was gone. My colleagues were putting pressure on me to date or "get a man." Most of them were married and had children. That seemed to be the "right" life. I just wanted to teach, coach, and run.

Boy, did I spend a lot of time running. I ran a 5K in the morning and a 10K at night. So, it didn't seem odd that I was losing weight. I wasn't trying to. I was trying to run away from intimacy.

Being different before in my life I had always been creative. Like with reading and spelling. In high school my friends were black, and I let them believe ALL white girls did any weird things I did. In college, I lived with guys and they assumed I was a lesbian basketball player. My basketball teammates assumed I was involved with one of the guys I lived with. I never said a word and that made it easy to stay very unknown and "safe."

HITTING A WALL

Getting cancer was like hitting a wall I never saw coming.

It wasn't like my declining health was obvious. I was running and losing weight. My colleagues started to wonder if I was too thin. I was also struggling with shooting pain around my right ovary. When I initially went to see my doctor, they suggested I might have an eating disorder and thought I should see a therapist.

The idea was terrifying. I had no memories of my past.

My lack of any intimate relationship caused an immediate concern for the doctor because, apparently, unspoken to me, I had some scar tissue that presented some type of sexual activity. Things got more complicated when further testing revealed scarring and old injuries in my vagina that I had no way to explain. This just led them to the conclusion it was some psychological reason for my health issues.

I felt so helpless. Therapy just seemed like more questions. I was uncomfortable in the sessions. Finally, I got angry, "I don't know what the hell happened to me — stop asking!"

I broke into tears, and this may well have been one of the first times I'd cried since I was very young. I couldn't stop crying. That same night I woke up and remembered being in a puddle of blood. I was four. Suddenly, the entire memory surfaced in fullness.

I called my therapist and shared. I'd been raped when I was four. It was all very graphic and real. I felt relief when I finally got the story out. I thought for sure this must be what was wrong with me and maybe I'd get better.

My therapist encouraged me to go back to the doctor. Maybe it was worth checking my physical health now that I was working through the past. My doctors ran a battery of tests. The results were shocking. I had stage four non-Hodgkin's lymphoma.

I thought I had finally figured out that my issues were more psychological but no. Instead, now I was fighting on two fronts: physical and emotional. I had terrifying nightmares and new painful memories, and a cancer that was rapidly attacking me in the present.

Still, I'm a fighter. The cancer gave me something serious to fight against. I was determined to beat the cancer. Plus, it took all of my attention.

With the memories surfacing from the past, I wasn't willing, or able, to connect with my family. The cancer had revealed my blood type was AB-. Why that's interesting is AB- is incompatible with O, my father's blood type. Suddenly, the John I thought was my biological father couldn't be. That broke down any options for family support. It brought up more questions and pain from the past. No one in my family wanted to deal with me and those issues. I didn't know how to share what was happening with my colleagues.

I felt very alone.

I went through the first round of chemotherapy. I found the treatments slowed me down, but I could still run. My energy dropped, and I was feeling weaker and more vulnerable. I found my courage in simply pulling on my sweats and lacing up my runners and standing in my doorway looking outside.

At 23, I wasn't about to let the treatments take me away from the one path where I'd always excelled — sports. My running shoes were a statement of my aliveness. Lacing up those shoes each morning, going to my doorstep, opening the door, walking out to the trail, and standing was how I stayed sane.

Then round two of chemotherapy came. Things got a lot worse. I was much sicker. Being in my twenties, without family or support around, was hard. The friends I did have were frightened by the possible dying aspects of my illness. They stayed away. I can't say I blamed them. I was scared too.

I wasn't sure I had it in me to keep fighting. The cancer treatments were not going well. I had already had pneumonia once and almost died. I was scaring any life left in me with traumatic flashbacks from my childhood. My reality didn't fit my family's, which just made me feel crazy.

After a night of very little sleep and no one to call, I decided I wanted to end this insanity. There really wasn't much thought to the plan. As a cancer patient, I had lots of different pills. Surely there had to be some that didn't go together well. I searched my bottles and finally picked a few.

I opened each bottle. I opened my hand and poured several from each bottle into my hand. I got a big glass of water and started swallowing. I did this for two large fistfuls of pills.

I wanted to be outside before the drugs set in. I took my running shoes out to the porch and sat down to tie them up. As I was tying my laces, I had this very strange thought: *"Damn, I cannot die before I learn how to tie my laces right!"* It was loud and persistent.

I stood up, went back inside, and called my friend Barb.

"Barb, I just took a mess of pills. But I don't want to die yet." Barb was a bit frantic, feeling helpless, and said she'd come right over.

Due to all my chemotherapy, I was good at vomiting. I made myself throw up most of the pills. When Barb arrived, we went to the emergency room where my oncologist met me. They pumped my stomach and fortunately, instead of being thrown into a psych ward for suicidal tendencies, I was given my freedom as long as I went home with Barb.

This suicide attempt woke me up.

I wanted to live, and I had a tiny inkling into how I wanted connection. I had reached out to Barb. I had asked for help.

Okay, I was not quite ready for much connection — that part was going to take longer.

On the way back home with Barb, I shared my desire to do this living thing differently. Barb was a bit of an odd duck herself and made the comment, "Okay, but I'm not sure I trust you. We just left the hospital and you want to go back to your place — really — no way."

"Okay — but I know how I can keep myself safe." I told her about the shoelaces.

"I'm not ready to learn to tie them right yet — but I have an idea. Can we stop at a shoe store?"

Barb was curious and found a running shoe store. We walked in and I found the solution —

Velcro shoes.

No laces.

Barb got it. I committed to only wearing Velcro shoes until my treatments were done, and I got better at honestly relating and asking for help.

Those Velcro shoes took me through many more nightmares and some tough treatments.

I had a daily reminder right there on my feet that I wanted more out of this life.

CONNECTION DIDN'T COME EASY

I have my sisters and my stubbornness to thank for saving me. Sure, it hurt when their friends would laugh at me and damn if I would ever let them see me cry. Back then, there was no path to vulnerability for me. I'd locked that up tight. Who knew that little twist was my signature to someday finding a way back home.

I still tie my shoes backwards, not because I am concerned about suicide. I let go of the Velcro running shoes when I moved to Canada. That is when I really committed to opening myself up and connecting honestly to others about who I was. I don't need my backward laces to remind me that I want to live.

8.

Dying Is Not Dead

The day started with a jolt. My alarm was so loud it was rocking the table. I grabbed it and stuffed it under the covers hoping to avoid having to get up. I felt crappy. I knew it was that time in my cycle when I would be lucky to have the energy to get through the full day working in the operating room (OR).

Still, the muffled sound of the clock, and the vibrating sheets were calling me out of my lousy self. I wanted this job as an OR technician. I needed to pull myself out of bed and shake off the doom and gloom and get going.

I had been working in the OR for a few months now and enjoyed my job. Sure a six a.m. start time was a drag, but I was grateful to have the position.

I didn't come to this job the normal way. No, I had been a physical education teacher when I was diagnosed with cancer at the age of 23. Due to the treatments, I had to go on long-term disability. However, I still wanted to give back. I took a job at a daycare ... for a day. I was too exhausted to work longer. Unfortunately, that one day working lost me my long-term disability benefits. Here's how I handled that.

EARLIER

Walking into the hospital administrator's office I wondered what I thought I was going to accomplish, but then again, I had nothing to lose.

"Can I help you?"

"Yes, I am here to talk to Jonathan Wells."

"Do you have an appointment?"

"No, but I can wait if he is busy. I came early hoping to catch him before he got too busy."

"Can I tell him who you are and why you're here?"

"I'm Susan Clarke — I am a patient — well, sort of — it's complicated. I was hoping not to have to go through this twice."

The assistant picked up the phone and signaled for me to sit.

"No. I am not sure why she's here, but she did say she was a patient — okay. I will tell her you'll get out shortly to see her."

Okay — step one done. Now for the harder part.

Jonathan Wells was a tall, very serious-looking gentleman. When he stepped through the door, I made sure I got to my feet to shake his hand.

"Susan — I hear you would like a word with me and aren't interested in sharing your story twice so come on in." His smile surprised me. Maybe I had simply assumed a serious man.

"Thank you for seeing me." The office was large with a big walnut desk taking up most of the space. There were a few smaller chairs on one side and a comfy desk chair that looked well-worn behind the desk. I sat in one of the smaller chairs — on the edge of my seat. He moved to the comfy chair and sat back, looking at me.

I started talking very fast, "Okay — so here's the deal. I started chemotherapy treatments here a few months ago. I have non-Hodgkin's lymphoma. I made the mistake of trying to work. So, I lost my long-term health insurance. I can't pay for the treatments anymore. I want to work for you and get my treatments..." I wasn't about to slow down.

"I am an emergency medical technician. I've worked on a rescue squad and as a respiratory therapy technician through college. I can do a bunch of different things. I saw where you needed an anesthesia technician. I want to apply in exchange for my treatments." I was gasping for breath.

"Okay, maybe I should stop talking now." The smile was gone and Jonathan Wells, hospital administrator, was leaning forward, just staring.

I thought, *This cannot be good.* Silence.

He said, "We do have a position in anesthesiology that needs someone with EMT experience. You can apply for the job, and if accepted, we'll exchange your pay for your treatments."

I applied and got the job. I started working as an OR technician. My treatments continued.

BACK TO THAT DAY

I had just gone through a battery of tests to determine how well my treatments were working. I was on my second protocol of chemotherapy. I was confident. I wanted to make sure I kept this job. I had to get out of bed.

When I got to work at six a.m., the morning OR schedule was light. My cancer doctor called me and wanted to see me at one p.m. It seemed I could make that happen easily. Then the action started.

"Incoming" — a call from the ER. There was a woman coming in who had fallen from her porch and landed on a fence post.

"Possible abdominal bleed. Prep the OR." That was me.

A woman in her twenties was wheeled in by the EMTs. Her stats were stable but dropping. She was still talking and there was no outward bleeding. A line was already in place.

My job was to stay with her until the doctor arrived.

"I'm Susan."

"Jessie. I'm okay, right? I need to get a message to my folks. They are arriving. It's my birthday. I was getting my apartment ready."

"Jessie, I'm sure we can notify your family. Right now, you just need to focus on relaxing. How old are you?"

"28." She looked like she was fading.

"What do you do?" No answer. Just a mumble.

Trying to rouse her. "I need to let them know."

The doctor came by. "Let's move her to the OR. Vitals are dropping. Get three bags of O blood stat!!"

In the OR, everything happened quickly. At first, the

commands were normal. "Drape the body. I'm getting ready to make an abdominal cut." But soon blood was everywhere.

"Aorta puncture — more blood stat!!" the surgeon shouted.

"The bleeding is intense. We have to try to stop the bleeding. Call for cardio."

"The heart stopped. Get me an epi — now."

"No response. I'm pumping the heart. Damn it." After a minute or so he called it.

"Nothing — she's gone."

Just like that. Jessie was dead. Only moments ago, I'd been talking to her about her parents, her birthday. She was gone. I was in shock. The surgeon stood next to me.

"We had no idea she had punctured her heart. There was nothing we could do once we opened her up."

"But she was just talking to me."

"Yes — she was alive. Her body was in shock. She had no pain really. But we are not set up for that type of trauma. Though even downtown they'd likely not have been able to save her. Are you okay?" He took off his glove and put his hand on my shoulder.

"Yeah — but..." I was crestfallen.

Then, Sally, the anesthesiologist, called through the door, "Susan, it's 12:55 — don't you have a doctor's appointment?"

"Yes, right. I'm on my way."

I headed straight to my doctor's office. Down a floor. Dr. Cain was always on time. I knew I should move along.

"Susan, she'll be with you in a minute," the nurse said.

I was still shaking from the morning and running down. I was happy to take a seat.

"Okay — head on back, Susan."

When I walked in, I could tell Dr. Cain wasn't having a great day either. Normally, she'd make a joke or something. She was sitting behind her desk and looking at a file. I assumed mine. When she looked up, her eyes looked sad, heavy, and moist.

"Susan — sit down. I wish I had better news. This is really not what we were hoping for."

I could tell she was struggling.

"The results aren't good. You aren't responding to the treatments."

I could hear everything she was saying and knew this was very bad. But I felt numb. The words were simply going in but not settling.

"We don't have another option."

Pause.

"I have to be frank..." Long silence.

"You need to know that if things continue at the current rate of growth and spread, you *only have about six months to live*." That last phrase reverberated in my body.

She coughed and swallowed. I was still silent and numb.

"Did you hear me? Is this something you are able to hear? Say something," Dr. Cain insisted.

All that came out was, "I'm dying, but I'm not dead."

She looked at me confused. "Well, yes, that is true. You're not dead, but I'm telling you: Nothing we're doing is stopping the speed at which the lymphoma is advancing. I need you to know, Susan, I am saying *we don't have another option.*" She emphasized that last bit.

I was still thinking of Jessie being alive talking to me and now being dead. Then I was hearing Dr. Cain share this bad news about my treatments.

I just kept coming back to, *I may be dying, but I am not dead yet. Jessie is.*

"Look, I get your message … I had a rough morning. This woman, Jessie, died in the OR today. Yet she was alive and talking to me just before. Now she is dead. I get you're telling me I'm dying. But thinking of her, well, I may be dying, but I am not dead yet. Somehow it helps me."

I got up to leave.

Dr. Cain responded, "We can talk."

"No, I need to go. I hear you. I am dying. I'll set up another appointment."

I walked out and through reception. As I walked out, I spotted a flyer for a workshop: *Elizabeth Kubler-Ross's Life, Death, and Transitions*. I figured, Well maybe I should figure out how to die. I picked it up and walked out.

I wrote Elizabeth Kubler-Ross. I explained that my doctor wanted me to get more comfortable with the idea of dying. I saw her workshop and thought it might help. Though I had no money, I'd like to attend her workshop.

She wrote me back and accepted me and provided a scholarship.

I had no idea who Elizabeth Kubler-Ross was. You may not know, either. It didn't take me any time to find out. Turns out she's an expert on the emotional stages of death and dying: denial, anger, bargaining, depression, and finally acceptance.

When I arrived at the retreat center, there were 92 people, 90 healthcare professionals and two of us with cancer. I was overwhelmed. These practitioners loved Kubler-Ross.

Elizabeth was a small Swiss woman who was a force of nature. She launched into talking about the importance of emotions and releasing feelings. She commented how people were most reluctant to express anger. She believed expressing emotions has everything to do with health.

The retreat was experiential in nature.

Within a very short time, people started doing anger work. This was very strange to me. I wanted to run. Apparently I did not run fast enough. Instead, I checked out — out of my body. Next thing I know that little force of nature, Kubler-Ross, is yelling in my face.

"Get back here. NOW!"

I suddenly was aware of being in a small rolled up position on the floor in a corner. No idea how I got there or how long I'd been there. But her yelling got me present.

She helped me up, and we went to a small room.

"Look, you have some work to do if you want to live. I need to be frank with you — okay?"

"Sure." At that moment, I was still terrified of this small woman yelling at me, so I was pretty willing to let her say anything.

Her voice was soft and kind now.

"Here's the deal — there's no difference between you and me. But someone told you were dying. Truth is, I could be hit by a bus tomorrow and die. But because I haven't a clue what is going to happen, I am focused on living. You are focused on dying. You need to shift that."

It was like a light went on inside me. I remembered Jessie. I remembered my own knowing — I am dying (we all are) — but I am not dead.

Suddenly, I was so alive and awake. All I could say was, "Thank you."

Had Jessie not died in the morning — I likely would have never picked up that flyer. I would have only heard I was dying — or dead.

It was a tough moment, but one that is always with me. As is Kubler-Ross and her reminder — live fully — not focused on dying, living!!!

Kubler-Ross launched me on my path to living and my life-guiding motto:

Choose to live. Choose to be curious. Fearlessly or fearfully face whatever is in front of you. Do not step away from chaos, conflict, and uncertainty. Instead, step in and reap the magic and the miracles.

9.

Arrival Gates, Hospitals, and Churches: Why My Legs Are My Best Feature

I was surprised the first time I watched the movie *Love, Actually.* The opening scene in the airport with Hugh Grant sharing the wonder of people greeting family and friends! How that ritual was love, actually.

Well, before the movie was made I discovered for myself the wonder and inspiration that comes from sitting at the arrival gates in the airport.

In my early twenties, I was dealing with aggressive cancer treatments. The treatments were one form of hell, but as I was wrestling with fighting cancer, I had also uncovered and cracked the illusion of my happy childhood. Scar tissue and the announcement of my blood type that was incompatible with my father's had been thrown in my face. I asked and searched for some answers. What I found instead of answers were nightmares and fragments of a story twisted with evil, lies, and an amazing cover-up.

That period of my life was what unearthed what I call my crazy. It may have also reawakened my creativity.

I couldn't sleep through the night. As night approached, I would find it impossible to close my eyes. I was scared I might not wake (the cancer) or I'd simply have another new terrifying fragment of the past surface. Nights were especially long!

Because I knew that at night I would be wrestling with why I wanted to live. I would do whatever I could to find some form of inspiration.

Sometimes just putting on music would work. I loved listening to the tunes of John Denver — "Rocky Mountain High," "Poems," "Prayers and Promises," and "Looking For Space" — were a few favorites.

However, sometimes I just couldn't shake my despair and my feet would take me out the door and to the arrival gates. Now you need to know this was well before 9/11; the arrival gates were right there, and you could watch people walk off the plane and be greeted by their loved ones.

I would sit there and watch. In my mind, I imagined a day when I felt that joy and love again. That day when I had dear friends or family meeting me at the gate or me meeting them.

Sometimes as I sat and watched, I would feel a tear roll down my cheek. At that point in my life crying did not come easy. One tear sliding down my cheek felt amazing. I knew I could still feel and that I still had some faith in humanity.

When I watched *Love, Actually* make the airport ritual a universal expression of love through those hugs and greetings, I felt joy and resonance.

Of course, the airport in the middle of the night doesn't have quite the right level of traffic, but I discovered that hospital cafeterias are always open. After a little time at the airport, I'd crash in the hospital cafeteria. People were not generally as joyful, but the common link was usually some deep emotion and connection.

I never quite found the same inspiration, say, if I went

grocery shopping at two a.m. — sure, there were people, but it wasn't the same.

Arrival gates and hospitals have something in common. People are there because someone they love is arriving or someone they love may be dying. These two moments cut to the root of what matters — letting people know you love them and making contact.

I don't believe I understood my natural compass to find just what I needed to give me hope but somewhere inside my being I did know. I give my feet and legs most of the credit.

Over those years of wrestling so closely with life, death, and demons, I would be at a place of giving up and my feet would take me somewhere where I'd find a reason to wake up again.

CHURCHES

I wasn't really a churchgoer, but one thing I love to do in places where I don't know anyone is walk into a local church, especially during Christmas.

Where I lived in Virginia, the churches were mostly black Baptist. When I walked through the door, people would stare but within a few moments someone would welcome me. Usually with a hug. That always amazed me, not a lot of words, but a true welcome.

However, what I really loved was the singing and the full-embodied spirit of these churches. That is what drew me in. Sometimes I'd sing along, stand and move to the songs. I loved when I felt the music; I could breathe in that deep faith. I love voices that allow me to feel that spirit in my cells.

I can't say all churches are alike. Many to me are missing that embodied spirit, the walls aren't rocking and filled with grace. Instead, people seem still and stiff. In those churches, my feet usually walk me back out. I like to feel faith through my cells — not just hear it in words.

Over the years, I haven't had the same need to tap into a reason to live. I no longer walk the streets at night fearful of dreams or dying. But sometimes life does present challenges that cause me to lose faith. These days instead of airports, hospitals, and churches — I head to the dog park.

I have discovered the joy of just hanging out at a dog park whether you have a dog or not.

I knew I wasn't going to be ready to get another dog until my health and life were really back in some sort of order. I also know dogs are heart defibrillators for me. When my heartbeat is either out of rhythm or threatening to ice up and stop, a drive to the dog park is one sure way to get things back on track.

There is just something about watching dogs play and discover how to be with each other that is inspiring. Plus, dogs love their people unconditionally — there's that love again.

Over the years now, I have had four amazing dogs put their paws on my heart and ensure my heart keeps beating!

But dogs may be a different storyline than airports, hospitals, and churches.

Back to my legs and feet.

I am grateful for my legs and feet. I have always thought my legs were my best feature. Though until writing this piece I thought it was simply because they looked good.

But really my legs and feet always knew when to walk.

Somehow my feet could interrupt the talk in my head.

Be it running, taking me to an arrival gate or a late-night hospital cafeteria where I would be reminded of what really matters in life — my legs have always been my greatest ally and I am so very grateful.

10.

Heaven and Hell: How All This Started

HEAVEN: FREEDOM

"She's going to drown. Stop her!" I heard my mom's desperate voice.

Splash.

I was in. Kicking with both my arms and legs underneath the water. Determined to swim across the lake. The water was cool, dark, and deep. I just kept paddling for all I was worth. My head was remaining well above the water with all motion happening beneath the surface. I could hear the commotion back on the dock. But I was going for the buoys that marked my turnaround point.

"She's only *three*! She can't possibly swim that far."

"Help her!"

"Do something!" Words without faces, fading background.

More motion, nothing was going to stop me. I didn't care if someone swam alongside. I was just kicking and paddling for all I was worth.

I grabbed the buoy, it popped me, and I turned about. No stopping, just kicking, no holding on, just grab, turn, and go.

"Thank goodness, she made — oh no — she is swimming

back — STOP HER!" My poor mom yelled.

I looked. No one was close.

I was on the home stretch, I could see people gathered. What was the big deal?

"My god, she is going to make it!" Someone in the crowd commented.

"Damn, I did not see that coming. I'll make sure she knows better."

"Just get her out of the water."

A hand reached out and pulled me in one motion up onto the dock. My mother picked me up in one of the few hugs I ever remember.

"Are you crazy? You could have drowned!"

These were just words. What I remember was the hug, the tight hug, triumph, and the feeling both of having done something awesome and horrible at the same time.

I was three and had made my big move, running from the shore to the deep-end dock. Jumped. I had watched others gain their freedom to swim anywhere with that move and I was certain I could as well! I wanted to swim. I wanted to take the lake! So I ran and jumped and did the only thing I knew how to do — dog paddle. Over 200 yards out to the buoy and back.

Camp was like that, 600 acres of land and water for me to explore and discover. I was free. I took chances. I jumped.

HELL: DESOLATION

"You can trust me." Big blue eyes, soft still like water.

Stabbing pain, smothered. Sinking, sinking. I can't breathe and all I feel is intense, stabbing pain.

"You can trust me — be calm." And the blue eyes, no longer soft. Intense. I am scared. Pain, pressure, and those big blue eyes.

Something ripped inside.

Suddenly, warmth spreads through my body. The stabbing pain stops. Liquid is surrounding my body and the warmth is penetrating through the numbness.

There is only light radiating, and I am drawn towards the light. As I drift away, I see from above the pool of spreading blood and the small frame of myself stripped from the waist down. Still and small. He is holding me in his arms.

We were playing out in the fields. No doubt some game involving the elements, either creating a fort or building lakes and waterways from the rain. The summer days were filled with these types of activities. We had the run of the camp as the youngest kids. The camp director's daughter, BJ, and I, the nurse's youngest — best of friends and at times competing enemies for the attention of those older.

I needed to pee and knew the closest, was BJ's house.

I ran into the unlocked house as though it was my home. Down the hall to the long bathroom to the toilet all the way at the back. My legs swinging from the seat when I heard his voice.

"Susie, is that you?"

I flushed, as I saw that I'd left the door open and it was only a matter of minutes before he would find me. Maybe I could stay silent.

"There you are." No escape.

"Come with me." He was moving toward me with his hand out. I jumped to my feet, pulling up my shorts without wiping and moved toward him.

He scooped me up in his arms. His arms, strong and muscular, easily swinging me and setting me down on the end of the bed. His smile and his eyes drew me in. I was always ready for one of his stories. He pushes me back on the bed and pulls off my pants.

As I look down at myself now, I notice he is not holding me but pumping forcefully against my body. My small body, limp and surrounded in a pool of blood. That warm liquid that is continuing to spread. He pulls away and wipes the liquid that came from him. He walks from the room. I am alone.

"*I am here.*"

Deep melodic voice. A beautiful sound coming from the light. I am drawn further from the limp shell now totally alone.

"I am always here."

"It is not yet your time. But I will stay for now. You can remember me any time."

My eyes close.

Suddenly awake. Lying in a hospital bed.

"She fell from a tree. Landed on a limb. Just horrible." Voices no faces.

"She is lucky he found her in time."

I keep my eyes closed. Not yet ready to let them know I am back. Who is he? Is he the voice I heard? Where am I? I don't remember falling from a tree. All I remember is, *"You can trust me"* and pain.

They turn as someone is entering the room.

"You're back. We were just saying how lucky this little girl was you found her."

I slowly open my eyes. All I see is his muscular arms, and I can't breathe.

No — no, I feel cold and still again.

"Would you like to sit here until she wakes up? I am sure she will want to see you when she wakes."

Please no. I am alone.
Desolation.

11.

Two Johns

HEAVEN: THE BEST OF JOHN

The fire crackled as the story was coming to a close.

> *"Wicked John, you know you ain't got a place here. My boys, they tried to help you. Now you are on your own." The devil himself passed a hot sack of coals to Wicked John through the iron gate.*

> *Wicked John, he took those coals off into another part of the woods. That's why sometimes late at night you might see off in the trees the burning embers. Well, that's Wicked John — in his special place.*

He stood and took a long look around. He had the stage in that flickering flame. From start to finish. Not a word spoken, not a challenge from anyone.

He paused in the silence, then nodded his head and headed back up the trail.

I could feel the shiver around the circle as he walked away. The fire flickering and each of us wondering if we would see Wicked John this week.

I loved listening to him tell a story.

Each week, at the start of a new session, by the campfire

he would come and tell one of his tales. All were gathered, young and old.

It was one of my favorite summer evenings and "Wicked John and the Devil" was one of his best.

That was the best of John — the storyteller.

No doubt it's where I fell in love with tales and words and ways to give things light.

HELL: THE OTHER SIDE OF JOHN

If there's heaven, though — there must be hell!

As with most things that shine so bright — there's often darkness in that light.

The heat inside of me was burning. I couldn't speak. Red hot rage was bubbling through my insides. From somewhere, I heard —

"Susie, are you okay?"

It was like a voice coming from far, far away. I wanted to answer. "No — he..."

But the words were stuck deep in my throat, blocking my ability to breathe. I walked further down the hall and suddenly I stopped, turned, and punched my fist right through the wall. I could breathe again. But still no words.

"What the hell? Why did you punch a hole in the wall?" My father's voice was now clear. He grabbed my arm, pulling it out of the plaster and me away from the wall.

"Why? Why? Why? Explain yourself." I have no idea if he really said why more than once.

"Explain yourself!" And the lump started to return.

"I ... can't..." The words were muffled and spoken to the floor. I could not look up or even make an effort to pull away.

"Bernie, do something with her. There is no way this is okay. She is too angry."

I wanted to speak. I wanted to say —

"I am furious. And that is okay."

The puppies had been born beneath the long house at the junior end of the Camp. BJ and I almost always took the path by that long house on our way to the lake. We had discovered the puppies by accident one day.

"They need food." I wanted to pick one of them up. But they were all piled together and though I longed to cuddle one of them, I knew enough that the best thing at this point was to let them be. See if their mom returned. Maybe we could bring some food, milk, or something.

"They are adorable. But they can't be here. Not once camp opens. Let's come back with milk. If their mom hasn't shown up — we'll do something," BJ said.

BJ and I were best buds, her dad was the camp director and my mom the camp nurse.

Every summer since I was two, we would come and spend the summer months at the camp. Shared summers, shared June birthdays, we were like twins with totally different personalities. She was quiet and nice (though I knew she had a bit of a wild side), and I was hyper, loud, and always into something.

The mom did not return. Often, I came alone because we didn't want anyone to know what we were doing.

I would come and visit at least four times a day. They were growing fast, and if I simply sat down on the ground they would come tumbling out, rolling all over me. Sometimes, I'd bring along a bag or a string. They loved playing. One of the smallest was always behind, but he was my favorite. I nicknamed him Bubba — not even BJ knew that. Being small, playtime was quick to result in a nap and a puppy pile. I would simply throw down a towel and spoon the whole pack of them. Definitely some of my favorite moments. I wasn't usually one to be still, but with them, I would settle right down.

The puppies were healthy and doing well. Two days before camp opened, we had a plan to take them to the pound.

I found myself humming as I came up to the long house that day, that day that started so well — that day that camp went from heaven to hell.

There he stood.

"Didn't think I knew about these!" He was holding one of them up by the tail. The little fellow was wiggling, and he just whacked it until it was still.

I went right at him. All 60 pounds of me, right into his chest, punching. He tossed the puppy and grabbed me by the neck.

"Let me be clear. The puppies might have been just fine. But you need to learn a lesson, and let's just say, you're like these puppies. You need to know I will destroy anything and everything you care about."

He picked up another puppy with his free hand and threw it against the wall of the long house. The puppy was still.

"Now watch." He had me in a neck grip. I could not fight. He grabbed a burlap bag and started tossing the puppies into the bag. With me in one hand and the bag in the other, he pushed me towards the lake.

"BJ thinks I am taking the puppies to the pound. Let's keep it that way." He took the bag and held it underwater. I watched — I wrestled but could not move. I wanted to scream, but nothing would come out. The water moved and then was still. The puppies were gone.

So was a part of me.

He didn't let go of my neck until we were back, close to the lodge. My mother was coming out of the cabin.

"You guys off on a lake hike?" she asked.

"You know Susie, loves the woods and the trails. Thought I'd show her some of the best parts of the lake. Wasn't that

fun?" He sounds so kind.
So sincere.

I was silent. I was furious.

I didn't speak. I walked into our cabin. Heard the voice.

"Susie, are you okay?"

Far, far away.

Did an hour pass? A day? I don't know. I don't know. I just know the puppies died.

I was furious and silent in my rage.

I put my fist through the wall.

PUPPIES TO PILLS

"Susie, talk to me. Help me understand why you are so angry." The man seemed nice enough, but no way was I talking.

I sat silent.

"Okay, I am going to suggest that your parents start you on a low dose of medicine. This is designed to help you relax so you won't hurt yourself or anyone."

Silence.

The medicine just made me numb. The pain of the puppies gone.

The wonder of the storyteller lost — or so I thought.

12.

Get The Fuck Away From Me!

"Get the fuck away from me," I screamed. My back against the wall, the chair gripped in my hands, the legs pointed at the intern and the nurse as my last line of defense.

"We just need to get a blood draw. All patients have to comply." The intern sounded so calm and rational.

"Susan, this may have nothing to do with you, but someone has been taking drugs," the nurse said adding more reasons why to what seemed totally insane to me.

"Don't come any closer! I checked myself in here. I will walk myself out. Get my doctor!" I was still holding the chair up and determined to use it if I had to.

I had checked myself into the psych hospital, and now I was terrified I was not going to be able to walk out.

When my efforts to integrate my past story into my present world had resulted in my health turning around, I'd started to own the pieces of my past.

I started attending a sexual abuse survivors' group. Slowly, sharing little details of my past.

I even established a strong connection to one woman, Gloria. Her story so touched my soul. I found myself going and grabbing a tea and conversation with her after each meeting. Her courage just drew me in. We'd talk about our very different pasts and stories. I'd go home to my little solo apartment. She'd walk back out on the streets.

I did ask once if she wanted to come to my place. She said, "You know I have money. I just don't like walls."

That night I walked into my one-room apartment. The light on the phone blinking. I pressed the listen-to-messages button.

"Stop talking — you will wish you were dead!" The voice, not one I knew. My heart beat faster. Nausea. Silence.

I tried to steady my breath. This wasn't the first of these calls and the voices never sounded the same.

I sat down on my bed. A tear, the only clear sign of the scream happening on the inside.

The next day I went again to the meeting.

Gloria wasn't there.

I didn't stay. I had hoped to draw upon her courage.

As I walked my way home, I had an icky feeling. Gloria never missed. She'd said those were the only walls that were safe.

Out on the street, near my apartment, I saw an unfamiliar car. The windows were down and there was something about the car that wasn't right. I crossed the street and froze as I looked into the back seat.

Bound and gagged. Nude. Painted black and white. Gloria.

The note attached: Stop Talking

She wasn't dead. I called the police. 911. I took away the gag and held her in my arms until they came. No words. Shallow breathing and heartbeat.

They took her to the hospital. The police asked me if I knew her.

I said, "No."

I didn't want any more harm to come to Gloria. I knew

that note was for me. She did not deserve that.

I called my only solid, safe person. My therapist. I told her about the calls and now this. I was scared. I didn't want to live and have others die.

She met me and suggested I check myself into the psych hospital so I would stay safe. I nodded.

I talked to the doctor at the psych hospital with my therapist there. I said I'd agree to check in. I needed somewhere to be.

TWO WEEKS OF SAFE

There in the psych ward I learned the way around, the rules I had to follow. The drugs that got distributed. The conversations or groups you had to attend. Those people who were safe and easy to talk to, and those that were, let's just say — not so safe and easy to talk to.

I found the places where you didn't have to talk.

I found comfort in the safety of the locked doors.

I found safety in sharing my crazy.

I found ways to connect.

I started to want to stay.

No one here was telling me I had to make sense or share the whole story.

I just talked.

Notes were taken.

I knew that not much of what was written down was about the actual story. They were more worried about whether I was making sense. I knew as long as I didn't,

I could stay inside the locked and safe walls of the psych ward.

Then the day came....

"Susan, we have to draw your blood." She spoke in a calm, rational tone.

"You don't have a choice. This is what you agreed to."

The cost of safe haven.

THE COST OF CRAZY

I knew I couldn't stay in the psych ward. But I'd hoped to stay long enough to know what I had to do next.

I managed to get released. I walked out more shaken than when I walked in.

I had only recently returned from The Haven and committed to this journey of connection. I had the phone number.

"Can I come there?" I asked, voice trembling.

"Hold on. Well, I do know we did put you down as coming back for the phase program in a month. Let me see what's possible." I recognized Dianne's voice. Strong and solid. I hadn't signed up for any programs. I did have a slight memory of hearing that I was welcome to come back.

I had left The Haven assuming I was dying. I thought the invitation to come back was meant to help me on the road ahead.

"I will find a way to get there." I heard myself say. Not at all sure that was a possibility.

"Well, we'll figure out what to do with you when you get here. Travel safe, Susan."

I'm sure there were more words than this. I know that it wasn't a 24-hour turnaround. However, it all happened quickly.

Reality shifting again.

I walked away because I couldn't live where I was — no cancer — no crazy.

It was scary as hell walking from the world I knew. Not everyone ends up in a psych ward.

Cancer and Crazy did bring me to my knees and almost took me under.

I never did track down Gloria again.

I knew I couldn't help her. I knew I also could not let that note make me forever crazy, quiet, or dead.

Gloria deserved more than that.

Me too, for that matter.

Water and Rock

"Water is fluid, soft, and yielding. But water will wear away rock, which is rigid and cannot yield. As a rule, whatever is fluid, soft, and yielding will overcome whatever is rigid and hard. What is soft is strong."
– LAO TZU

My soul is like water.

We want to make our reality solid like rocks.
Stories that make sense, don't change.

However, our soul, our spirit is much more like water than rock.
Our soul is influencing and shaping us. Sometimes with gentle nudges.
Sometimes like white water.

Here's the deal.

Rocks, walls, and words can become solid and safe.
However, safety in words and walls can become cages.

I almost died from my solid structures.
My truths.
Water started rushing into my fortified structures.
The stories or stones that broke free and tumbled out seemed wild and crazy.

Fractals freed to shape and shift.
Fractals always threaten structure, at least sane, linear,
and safe ones.

Like roots rising through the cement sidewalk.
Hurricane devastating an entire housing area.
What is wild and free will not be contained.

Dying might have been easier.
My soul roared and blasted back.
My voice spoke.
I walked out of the safety of crazy.
Into a life unknown.

We all face those moments. Too often the death we choose
is slow, steady, and without warning.
Reality can seem like the rock, unyielding in a truth.
Water is ever present.
All around.

In nature
Inviting us to listen

Shifting reality
Moment to moment
Breath to breath.

Warm

A Short Prayer

Before I pass on into a new life
Help me to be at peace with this body
I have been at war
Fighting to conquer the pain
To be strong and indomitable
To move at a pace that never allows a moment of silence
To avoid ownership of my mother, my daughter, my
womanhood
I have fought well
For I have survived a great darkness
I have almost silenced the stirring between my thighs
Yet the blood still flows
There is a flame that still burns
In this circle of women, I am moved again to try to connect
To spend a few moments containing the paradox
Of agony in ecstasy
Life and death
The horror and the beauty
I know it is all there
In this body
In this heart
In this spirit
In our dance I am able to share my story
To hear yours and to know of our connection
For moments we are joined
And I am encouraged and inspired to continue
In these few days I have witnessed the beauty of womanhood

The incredible strength in the sharing of sorrow, laughter, and joy
I honor our experience in my prayer
In my words
So that tomorrow when I am drawn back into my war
I may know peace
Even if it is only for a moment.

13.

Finding Haven

"Susie, you ready for some needles?" Jock asking me about getting acupuncture.

"Sure," I replied without looking up from the carpet. Jock sat down beside me and started taking pulses (Chinese medicine pulses).

I had become a bit more comfortable with our routine now. Each session, since day one of the program Come Alive, Jock would come over and ask if I was ready for needles. I had never done any acupuncture before and for sure not in a room full of people. But everything about this Come Alive experience had been new, different, and very enlightening.

Today, though, I noticed a bit more of twinge and pinch as the needle went in. "Ouch."

"Take a breath," Jock encouraged.

As I took a deep breath in, suddenly tears and a choking sound emerged from my mouth. I bent further over and the tears were now in full flow. I thought I was choking and thought I heard Jock reminding me to just breathe. I also was aware of feeling very far away from his voice.

The next thing I felt was a big, salty, wet tear dropping on my face. I blinked and opened my eyes ever so slightly, looking up into Jock's eyes, where the tear had come from. He was holding me in his arms. Behind him someone had their back supporting him. As I peeked out from my cuddled position, I could see that the rest of our group was gathered around.

I don't remember being lovingly held even as a very young child and for sure not as an adult. Yet I did want to let this caring in and the felt sense of safety to last longer.

Slowly, I was aware of music playing and caught the eyes of Ben. The loving and tenderness in his eyes brought more tears to my own.

This was not what I had assumed Come Alive would be like — but wow, I did feel more alive and loved in that moment than I think I ever thought possible.

So how did I get into Jock's arms — well, let me take you back. Like maybe a couple months.

TWO MONTHS PRIOR

At some point in my cancer journey, I did come to terms with the idea that I was dying — and soon.

In many ways, the knowledge that I had limited time left on the planet was a big reason I finally decided I would surface the crazy memories of the past and talk about what I remembered.

When my sister, Penny, who lived on the other side of the country, called to say she would really like to have some time together, I wasn't altogether sure that was going to be the best time spent. Still, she wanted time together and wanted me to talk to a friend of hers, Janet, and maybe take a program called Come Alive that happened on a remote island in British Columbia, Canada.

At this point, I was well into the six-months-to-die countdown my doctors had given me, and a trip across the country seemed unlikely, but hell — why not talk to this friend, Janet?

Janet called me and we ended up talking for 45 minutes. She was a remarkable woman who had her own incredible story of healing. She also offered an interesting twist on why I might just want to sign up for Come Alive.

"Look, you two don't seem like you've really been all that close or aligned. I honestly can't imagine a week of just hanging out together is going to be much fun for either of you. But at Come Alive — well, it's a beautiful island. If nothing else, you'll each have a powerful experience and meet some interesting people. Ben and Jock are doctors and believe healing happens in groups, not hospitals. Plus, this is something to keep you each engaged, even if you don't get closer to each other."

That was a different pitch — and it worked. Why not? I had NOTHING to lose.

THE TRIP NORTH

Penny and I made the drive up from Seattle. What you need to know about The Haven and the home of Come Alive is that it happens at a small resort on Gabriola Island, BC. If you've ever read the book, The *Mists of Avalon* — well, that is what it is like getting to Gabriola. It's only 170 miles north of Seattle — but takes a minimum of six hours to get there. Going by car, there's a border crossing and two ferries that can make that timing even more interesting.

There's something magical and mystical about driving off the car ferry and down this beautiful two-lane road to The Haven. The lodge was built close to the water's edge. It's gorgeous looking out onto the Georgia Strait.

When we arrived, Janet ran out to welcome us. Though we had never met, her hug was warm, real, and like we'd been friends for years. We checked in and got the lowdown on the schedule for the next five days. I found the place sort of surreal. There was an old lodge that was rundown — yet cozy. The furniture was a very eclectic assortment of comfy chairs and couches around a fireplace, with a bar just around the corner on the other side. The dining area looked out over the water, but the ceiling and the framed window area was overrun with ivy growing through every crack.

Our room was a short walk from the lodge in another somewhat old and rustic building. Our room was dark and had just enough space to walk through the beds to the bathroom. The bedspreads and window curtains were anything but matching — but somehow that just made the space feel like home. It didn't take us long to spread our stuff out and settle in.

COME ALIVE

The name does this program justice. The next five days were simply transformative, and frankly, the single most healing, accepting, and relational work I've ever witnessed.

Though at the time, I wasn't quite ready for the reality of

the miracle that occurred. I'd never witnessed people being so real, honest, and raw. I also experienced what it was like to open, feel deeply, be witnessed, and accepted. Now, it wasn't always easy. We were presented with a way of communicating that demanded a deeper awareness and curiosity about myself and others than I'd ever considered.

Yes, I was a teacher and well-versed in education and to some degree psychology — but nothing like this. These people were working with the body, mind, and spirit all while relating to a circle of people with all sorts of backgrounds, experiences, and journeys. Each member of the leader team was so personal in their own sharing. It was hard not to want to attempt to be as real and straight about what was happening.

We each had some "personal exploration" time, and I was encouraged to go early since the two founders were physicians and had heard I was facing a terminal cancer process. They figured I could use all the breathing and support they had to offer.

Of course, my agreement to jump in did not result in an easy process. As I lay down on a mattress in the middle of the circle and was encouraged to breathe deeply, I totally spooked myself. I was encouraged to say, "Stop, Jock" or "Stop, Ben" if I wanted to end the process. I didn't last for more than a few breaths. I just wasn't ready.

"Stop, Ben. Stop, Jock." And I made my way to the wall and curled up tightly. I was still in the room and wanted to stay present, but my level of trust was very low.

That didn't stop any of the leaders from continuing to work with me. I found a place to sit against the wall through each session. This led to Jock, who did acupuncture, coming over while folks were gathering to offer me some needles. He'd sit beside me, encouraging me to keep working on my breathing and share a few stories while putting in those needles.

Day three Jock came over to do the needles. Suddenly, my tears started flowing — uncontrollably. At this point, I honestly don't remember ever crying since I was about 9 years old. It was like a floodgate had opened. I just collapsed and went with it. Next thing I remember, I felt this big, wet, salty tear land on my face. I looked up to see Jock. I was in his arms in the center of the circle.

That was the crack that really started letting the light in. I won't say I was healed, but I was much more open.

In those last couple days, I made connections with my sister and other members of the group that have lasted years and years. These were people I laughed with and cried with. I listened and felt their pain and my own in resonance. Within the circle much was shared, but that personal and real talk happened between sessions, over meals, and out in the hot tub at night.

The last night we had a dance. I have never danced and had so much fun. I was terrified of going home because now I truly did not want to die — I finally had a purpose — I wanted to get good at being real and relational.

THE CLOSING CIRCLE

The last morning, I was anticipating some good-byes and maybe some final suggestions on how to keep living what we learned.

Ben and Jock introduced their friend, Father Jack. A man came into the circle wearing his robes and looking very Catholic. The guys shared that they'd wanted to offer a healing circle for me and that was why they had invited Father Jack.

I was blown away. These people had already done so much, and now this seemed like a lot.

It was interesting what happened, because many people in the circle were not happy that a priest had joined us. A number had big issues with the Catholic church and religion in general. Things got quite heated. Father Jack just sat down in the circle and said, "Look, I get why you have issues with the church, and I'm willing to listen. I think we need to clear the air if I am going to stay. So, let's talk."

For a good 30 minutes, people really did vent and toss some strong anger toward Father Jack. He was quite something. He acknowledged some things he knew he himself had possibly done, and mostly he shared that these people had very solid reasons for being angry at the church and God. He said he felt badly about that.

He didn't defend or fight about it. He listened. I myself had not seen anger and conflict addressed with so much honesty, listening, and compassion.

In the end, everyone decided they wanted to stay and wanted Father Jack to lead the healing circle.

I felt so deeply touched by having witnessed this dialogue. I wanted to be as open and real as I had witnessed these people being. I sat in the center of the circle. People came forward and touched my forehead with Father Jack's holy oil. I found myself breathing in their tenderness, their caring. In that moment, I had a felt sense of every cell in my body responding.

I knew my cells had changed. Something deep had opened, and the light had come shining in.

RETURNING HOME

My sister and I drove home to Seattle. Laughing and simply in a place of joy.

I returned back to Virginia where I was scheduled to have a surgery the next day to remove the tumors that were filling my abdominal cavity. This was a procedure for eliminating the pain, though at this moment there was not a possible cure — just comfort.

I probably should have said, "I don't think I need that surgery." But I wasn't all that great at challenging my medical team.

One of my doctor's did say, "You look completely different."

I went in for the surgery — no tumors. That's right, the tumors were gone and so was any sign of any cancer. They had to take out my appendix to justify the surgery for insurance reasons.

I know — crazy, impossible, right?

Well, it happened.

The power of people's attention. The power of connection and even the power of conflict that is out, open, and addressed. That opening and willingness to feel deeply and connect through pain, through differences. That type of genuine contact is what loving really is. That genuine contact and loving is what takes us out of separation and into wholeness.

Miracles happen there.

The Haven went on to become my home and the place where I discovered living and relating.

There are not many ways to share those years and do it justice. Maybe my fairy tale written in those early days says it best:

Long ago, a young girl arrived at a grand kingdom. When she arrived at the gate, she was amazed at the beauty. The grounds were so beautiful and the people so kind. She was invited to come in. She sat at the table of kings and heard magnificent stories. She learned a great deal about how to care for the grounds and the people of the kingdom.

She was given the opportunity to share her own tales. The tales of her life and land. She found this very difficult. At first, she had trouble remembering about the land from which she had come. Her mind was filled with a darkness she did not understand.

Slowly, she found words for the shadows and a story unfolded. Many in the kingdom were troubled by the darkness in the foreign land of which she spoke. They wanted the kings to gather an army together and go fight the dark lords who had tortured the young girl. But the kings refused. Instead, they offered the young girl a permanent piece of land in their kingdom. They encouraged her to continue to tell her tale. To write, to sing, and to share her stories of the dark lords. Over the years, the young girl grew strong and skilled at caring for other people. Her stories became tales of dancing in darkness and light, and people found when they listened they were at first frightened but then inspired. Inspired to tell of their own darkness and their own dancing in the twilight.

The kings were happy. They themselves knew that every kingdom contained shadows and believed that the shadows only ruled when their stories remain untold.

Over the years of sitting and circles and sharing stories, I have witnessed many miracles happen when stories of darkness are shared and brought into the light.

14.

Power of Prayer

I'm back at another hospital, Seattle's Swedish Cancer Center. This time for some follow-up testing. I came down from British Columbia, Canada for what was supposed to be a brief one- or two-day visit. Nothing is ever that easy for me when it comes to medical testing.

Apparently, my six-month testing to make sure I was still clear of the non-Hodgkin's lymphoma had turned up a concern. I thought, *At least Swedish Cancer Center is a beautiful building. Instead of a basement oncology department, I get to be in a beautiful waiting area.*

"Welcome, Susan. We want to make this as easy as possible. So, I'll be around throughout the day to check in and make sure everything is going well. Hopefully, you will be done by day's end." Birgitta introduces herself. She is a volunteer staff that is assigned to a new patient. *Wow, nice touch.*

"Great. I was hoping to be heading home today and at the latest tomorrow. I'm staying with my sister, and I had promised this would only be a very brief visit just to validate the cancer is still gone."

I keep trying to push my departure up as early as possible. It's not that I dislike my sister. Penny is awesome. However, she lives on a houseboat. Besides, we have some family differences that are easy to avoid as long as our time together is short. Longer visits put more pressure on her to be the spokesperson to the rest of the family about how I am doing. The last time I spoke with my parents was difficult. As a result, I've pulled back and gone silent.

So today at the hospital, I'll have some blood drawn and an ultrasound. I am hoping that will provide enough information for my clean bill of health and my release.

"Come on back, Susan," a nurse calls from down the hall.

"The doctor will be in shortly." *Right.*

Surprisingly, she was right. He is, within minutes.

"Look, we have found a mass near your ovary that is a concern. The ovary is enlarged, and we need to do some more testing. We'd like you to stay for the week."

Damn. I knew it was too good to be true. My clean bill of health had only lasted seven months. I had recovered from a six-months-to-live diagnosis of non-Hodgkin's lymphoma. The battery of blood work on this trip was just supposed to ensure that cancer was clear. Now this. Ugh!

"I'm not sure. I had only planned for a day or two tops. I'll have to check. My sister wasn't expecting me this long, and she's got a small home."

"If housing is an issue, we have a program and volunteers who can help. You met Birgitta. She's one of a few folks we have that can help you find a place. Let me get her."

Birgitta came back into the room.

"Susan, I'm sorry about the delay in your plans. My husband and I do sometimes provide a temporary place for patients from out of town. I know this is very last moment — but I could check with him."

I had to admit, that sounded much easier than staying with my sister. Penny and I were just starting to reconnect; staying longer with her would create too much strain.

See, for several years while I dealt with my non-Hodgkin's lymphoma, I was estranged from my entire family. We had different versions of my childhood that I just could not reconcile. During that time, Penny and I had lived on different coasts. Until we reconnected by both attending a retreat together, which created a miraculous turnaround in my health.

Penny was going to have a hard enough time learning that I needed to stay for more testing. I wasn't at all sure my sister was going to be up for hearing that I might need another miracle. Finding a different place to stay to do this testing seemed like the best thing I had heard all day.

I responded, "Okay, but are you sure? You really do this sort of thing?" I had also stayed in a volunteer's home when I had treatments at the Mayo Clinic in Rochester. It seemed like "foster homes for patients." I never thought this was a common practice but was appreciating the support. I hated staying in hospitals. I preferred being in my clothes, eating at normal dinner tables, and sleeping in a real bed versus a hospital bed.

Birgitta explained that she lived on Bainbridge Island, just a ferry ride from downtown Seattle. She'd check with her husband and get right back to me.

As I sat there, I realized I'd love something to distract me from thinking about the new mass. I thought the cancer was gone. The previous treatments had been rough, most of which had taken place back east. Now sitting here in Seattle,

I couldn't help but think, *Why me and why now?* I thought I had turned this around. I thought I was done.

Birgitta came back with a smile. "Raymond is fine with you coming to dinner tonight. We'll talk then about how it might work if you stay with us through your testing."

On the ferry to Bainbridge, Birgitta shared that Raymond was a forensic scientist. He was engaged in criminal cases where he was responsible for pulling together the medical facts and forensic evidence for the state. He worked in downtown Seattle but enjoyed living on Bainbridge Island.

We met Raymond at a small Mexican diner. The place was tiny but awash with vibrant colors and delectable smells. Raymond stood up as soon as we walked in and shook my hand. He was a large man with a beard and a mustache wearing a dress shirt and tie.

"I'm Raymond, nice to meet you."

"I'm Susan Clarke."

His face changed as I said my last name.

"Do you have a sister named Penny Reid?"

"Yes, I do — Why, do you..."

His eyes welled up and his voice cracked. Suddenly, this big man was sobbing. He sat down with his face in his hands.

I wasn't sure what had happened. But I wanted him to have some space. I wasn't really sure if I wanted to know. I was a bit anxious myself.

"I'm going to find the bathroom," I said and wondered, *What could possibly make this big man cry?*

Birgitta looked surprised as well and signaled me to go.

When I came back, Raymond was still teary but much more settled.

"Please, I am so sorry. I just can't believe you are Susan Clarke. I am a scientist — and you are a miracle — let me explain.

"Four years ago, I was in a program called Context with your sister, Penny. I had spoken of being a practicing Lutheran. She asked me if I would pray for her sister who was dying of cancer.

"She had shared a bit about your situation and how you were not responding to treatments. She wanted all the help she could get. Well, sure, I was a Lutheran. So, I agreed to pray, but as a scientist I always questioned if this would do any good. I have always wanted proof that prayers were worth it. You, my friend, are my proof.

"I have prayed for you every day, every day for four years. I couldn't get your sister's story out of my mind. I just decided I was in for as long as it fit. I'd even ask God if there was any way I could help. If so, then give me a sign. Now, here you are. I had no other contact with your sister. I assumed you had died. Though, I had never checked and I wanted to keep praying. In my line of work, I need to believe in something. Now here you are, alive, asking if you can stay in my home."

I was stunned. Our lives had crossed paths in what seemed like a random act of kindness. Birgitta had no idea I was this person her husband had been praying for. I felt a tear roll down my cheek. Here was this man who had been pulling for me for no reason other than he wanted to believe in miracles. Even after he thought maybe I had died.

That is faith.

Raymond and Birgitta were angels in my life. I stayed

with them for a few weeks. I didn't get back to Canada for a while. This time it wasn't lymphoma, but an ovarian tumor. I did end up having surgery and then nine months of chemotherapy. Fortunately, Raymond's story gave me tremendous faith and joy. Plus, he agreed to keep praying, even after I moved on. I did feel like I was in good hands.

LIVING PRAYER FORWARD

Though I don't consider myself a religious person, I am a big believer in the power of prayer or intention.

I believe when one or more with open hearts extend energy, kindness, good will toward others, without attachment to the outcome or getting a pay back, it's good for the giver.

If by chance the receiver is open and willing to receive that prayer or intention, it is like an energetic dose of love and care. As helpful and powerful as any dose or medicine. In other words, amazing things can happen for all parties involved when a heart is open to giving and receiving.

I have a dear friend who years ago hurt her back and was stuck prone most of her days. She shared how she used her time just lying there — when someone would pop into her mind, she'd pray for them. She believes that prayer medicine gave her as much health and wellness as any other form of treatment. She walks now and still finds those simple prayer vibrations a vital part of her day.

I imagine many have received some powerful good vibrations from her. I know I have.

15.

My Fear of Fat

Recently, I stepped onto the scale and discovered that I had gained five pounds. I knew it'd been a while, and I'd been allowing myself some space to enjoy the Flathead Valley's craft beers and various Whitefish food fare.

I was also skiing regularly, was walking or running with my dog Rosie, and was diligent with my home yoga routine. As I digested the new number on the scale, I reminded myself that muscle weighs more than fat. Therefore, I didn't need to panic.

But within a few short minutes, panic was in full pursuit, screaming a need to fast immediately. I was ready to apply whatever sum of cash was required to get into a ten day cleanse, juicing experience, or something that would deal with my surfacing FEAR of FAT!

To distract myself, I turned to social media. As if in answer to my needs what should appear on my newsfeed but an advertisement with an incredibly buff woman in a fitness bra, tights, doing a move that required great strength and flexibility. What was loudest for me were her rock-solid abs and perfect dimensions. Right there on the ad was the statement: *The ten day yoga program that will make you look like this*!!

You may be thinking I signed up. But no — I blew up! I went into a full-on rage. Bullshit! Her body was not the result of any damn ten day program!

I really, really hate that type of ad campaign. It's possible that with her genes and diet, at some point, she did ten days of intense yoga that shaped her into something even better than she already was. She may even believe her yoga routine maintains her excellent balance between muscle mass and flexibility. Well, let's not forget her perfect bone structure, great hair, and flawless young skin. But I can tell you one thing for sure: No ten day program — be it yoga, fat camp, fitness boot camp — is going to transform my genes, scars, wrinkles, and body into that!

The idea that Facebook decided this advertisement was best for me pissed me off! However, this Facebook ad did knock some sense into me. I didn't make any radical decisions based on my Facebook feed or my visit to the scale. Nor did I rant and fire off hate mail to that perfect-looking yogini.

Instead, I decided it's time to face my FEAR of FAT! Not run. Not stop eating. Not do a new intense exercise program. But stop and face my fear.

What you need to know is I was a fat kid. Since the age of 11, I started putting on weight, and can honestly say, with a touch of flush as I write these words, that I weighed more between the ages of 12 to 14 than I ever weighed as an adult.

Not only did I have weight issues, I did *nothing* to improve my looks. In fact, related to clothing, hair, or make-up, I went the other way. I dressed more like a boy than a girl. My shoulder-length hair was either scrappy and full of tangles or cut short like I was wearing a soup bowl on my head. You could've read the invisible sign on my forehead that shouted: "Stay the fuck away from me!"

I know now that kid had a whole bunch of reasons for getting fat, keeping everyone away, and doing her damnedest to project, "Don't mess with me!" But I also know that young girl cared very deeply and had simply given up on humans.

Food was something that was comforting and relatively safe. Being called fat was simply a cost factor for a very reliable line of defense: fat, ugly, and untouchable.

Then I discovered sports. I was a pretty good athlete — a fat one but a good one. I could play a mean game of tennis, and when I decided to make sports my new refuge — hockey and basketball became favorites. I wasn't great, but I was determined, and underneath all that fat was some rock-solid coordination and tenacity.

Sports became my lifeline to human contact.

I soon discovered I could, with enough running and working out, stop the rising scales. I found a way to protect and guard myself that did not involve being fat! Exercise replaced food as a way to get far, far away from my fears, my terror, and my demons, which made it critical to not get too close to people!

However, back to our perfect yogini. Even at the pinnacle of my athletic career, which involved playing three sports and practicing four to five hours a day, I *never ever* looked anything close to her — NEVER!

With all my exercise, I ran myself smack into the hospital in my early twenties. I hadn't noticed I had lost almost 60 pounds, which tells you about my relationship with my body. At 5'6" I was just under 100 pounds.

You might be thinking, eating disorder, and there's some

truth to that. But the real factor of my weight loss was cancer. Yes, the fight to not feel my fear, my terror, and my demons had run its course.

Let me just say, in losing all that weight and even being very, very ill, I started to get lots of attention. Men suddenly found me attractive. I was bony and skinny and wearing a size six. I was a piece of nothing, but there's something about any woman that slender that attracts a certain response from men. I had never had that type of attention!

Sure, the dying of cancer wasn't so great — but skinny — well, there was something about that I liked.

Seven years later, after a clean bill of health from cancer, I realized I had a new problem.

I was terrified of going back to FAT! This new problem has now been going on for the better part of 25 years. I don't talk much about it. It's not like cancer. It's not the thing friends want to support you in facing. It's a bit like mental illness, which I could write about too, but I'll stick to fat.

When I saw the perfect yogini Facebook ad, my rage exploded. I let myself feel fully. The rage turned into a deep grief and I wailed.

Then I realized my fear of fat would never be resolved by being thin.

Being fat was not the problem. I'm not ugly, and I am not even fat. I do, though, have trouble feeling fully. I don't particularly like crying or feeling deep grief. Yet life, and being in relationship with people and this world, does offer a lot to feel deeply about, and it is not all happy and positive!

I won't be going on any radical diets or fasting for now,

nor will I go on a Facebook fast. I just need to be kinder to myself and maybe stop running and exercising so much to the point of not noticing when my body, heart, or spirit needs some attention.

I simply need to feel deeply.

My fear of fat is not over. But I am much more committed to turning toward the fear and facing it rather than running to get further and further away from myself and my feelings.

16.

Learning To Love My Fifth Grader

There are moments in life best to just forget. Right?

Often, those moments don't really go away. Instead, they lurk beneath the surface of our psyche, waiting to resurface, and play havoc.

For me, one of those moments occurred when I was in fifth grade in the early 70s in the inner city of Richmond, Virginia. My city school system was going through a LONG period of finding a solution to social injustice and racial segregation with the latest attempt to integrate.

The plan was to bus kids into an inner city building while a new school was being built.

The building I was bused to held only fifth grade.

There were about 350 fifth graders, 90 percent black and 10 percent white.

Looking back, I would definitely say there were some flaws in the thinking of the people who devised the plan. I also get the intense injustice and justified anger of the disenfranchised black students.

However, at the time, I was simply one of the 10 percent and determined to find a way to survive my first year of being bused out of my neighborhood and into a new school district.

I struggled. I was a young girl of 10 years, who apparently looked a lot like a boy.

DAY ONE

"Susie Clarke — are you here?" Ms. Childs, a tall and thin black woman standing in front of the classroom holding a clipboard, picked up her eyes to look for a raised hand as she went through the class list.

"Susie Clarke - where are you?"

"Here!" I called out.

"No, I said Susie. Do not start off on the wrong foot young man!" She said with a stern look.

"I am Susie. I am not a boy." I could feel a lump forming in my throat, as everyone in the class laughed, but I spoke with a determined strong voice.

No way was I going to show any tears.

Ms. Childs looked, and finally, after what seemed like an eternity, she checked me off.

That was the start of day one.

Things got worse.

Later that day Ms. Childs told me to come with her. She took me to the girl's bathroom. Then she asked me to pull down my pants to confirm I was indeed a girl. I was horrified but agreed. She was finally satisfied.

Though Ms. Childs created some of my initial problems with that opening day event, she also strongly encouraged me to stay positive, and not give up on my efforts to engage in making the school a better place.

CHARLOTTE — A GIRL ON A MISSION

Charlotte was one angry young girl. Clearly, she had good reason to be angry, growing up black in Richmond, Virginia.

Unlike many of the other black students, Charlotte took every opportunity to let me know she had the upper hand in this school environment.

When we had to be lined up in the hall, she'd slap me across the face. Then she'd remind me I should be in the back of line. I didn't belong upfront.

In the girls' bathroom, she'd push me into a stall. She'd tell her friends, "Behind this door is the boy playing a girl." She'd make sure I stayed put by leaning against the stall door, making it impossible to get out.

I wasn't her only target. Any light- or white-skinned person would attract her wrath, and it really didn't matter if a teacher was present or not. She was taking a stand against white people.

Charlotte was the ringleader of a gang of playground bullies who were relentless. Our playground was a two-block walk from the school, creating ample bullying time.

As a fifth grader, it was difficult to be the target. I took Ms. Child's advice to stay positive.

I decided to run for student council president under the platform of "no bullying."

We had the school event of speeches. I stepped up on that stage and said, "I am running because I want to stop the bullying." You could hear a pin drop, then there was a rolling, rising wave of laughter. Yet I was committed and thought I delivered a solid message and concern.

I talked to anyone who would talk to me.

I believed I had a chance to win and eagerly put my posters around. I didn't get flustered by any side comments or the popularity of some of the other candidates running.

VOTING DAY

I arrived early to cast my vote. Like any confident candidate, I put my vote in the ballot box with a check beside my name. Later, the principal came over the school's public address system to announce the winners. I thought he'd only list the winners.

No. He chose to read each name and how many votes they got.

I did not win.

I had one vote.

I knew it was my own.

I was horrified.

I slipped out to go to the bathroom.

Guess who was there?

Yes, Charlotte.

She grabbed me, spun me around, saw the tears, gave me a slap across my face, and started laughing.

"That will teach you white girl/boy — whatever."

I did manage to pull away and collapsed in humiliation and shame in the stall.

That crushing moment was seared into my cells.

I am not quite sure how I recovered.

I did get through fifth grade.

However, I did make a vow *to never, ever put myself in a situation where I was asking people to choose me ... Never step into that kind of leadership.*

Then I did what any good survivor does. I buried that moment.

The memory has stayed unearthed longer than other painful blows, many of which, on a physical level, were much worse.

What I didn't realize though is that memory has played havoc with my efforts to speak out with my own voice, to market my services, to write and share my stories.

Don't get me wrong, I have stepped out into leadership, but under someone else's platform. I lead other people's programs, and coach under the umbrella of other people's models.

More recently though, at thrive!, our consulting business, CrisMarie and I have been standing forward with our own voice and our own model.

I believe our ability to lean into conflict has made our relationship passionate, alive for over 20 years. We have each grown individually, as a couple and in our business.

Our platform is the beauty of conflict.

Hmm, someone could make the connection that making conflict beautiful may be about as popular as a white girl running on the platform against bullying. I really had not given that any thought until just now. (That may need some more processing.)

Selling the beauty of conflict hasn't been easy. No one likes conflict. Not even us, and we've written two books on it.

However, conflict is natural, normal, and creative. This is when used — which is what we help leaders and teams do. Bullying is really just conflict not being dealt with.

As we work on our marketing efforts for our business, and define our voice and brand, I have bumped into that old crippling doubt and unearthed roots of my fears: *fifth grade!* This book, *Crazy, Cracked, Warm, and Deep,* has taken forever to write and share. There are all sorts of reasons I wrestle with getting these stories out.

The various demons have all become little pieces of the book making their way out.

This damn book is only a tiny book, yet it has felt like the writing of centuries.

As I was coming to some sort of conclusion in assembling the book, guess who showed up?

No, not Charlotte.

My fifth grader: "Why am I not in the book? Are you still so ashamed of me?"

I listened. I turn toward that little eager, humiliated fifth grader. I am crying with her as I write.

My fifth grader deserves a chapter. This is her piece to the puzzle of me.

There wasn't any reason for me to be ashamed of my efforts in fifth grade.

As Brené Brown would say, *"I entered the arena."* It's okay that I lost, and I am glad I voted for myself.

I don't want to bury the moment. I want to release it. Share it.

No matter what the color of your skin, your economic status, sexual orientation, gender preference, I am guessing you've experienced a humiliating moment.

Maybe you buried that humiliating moment too, only to have it play havoc with some part of your life.

Don't bury it. Don't hide. Lead through it.

I will step up to lead with my voice.

I will ask people to choose me (and us).

Yes, I will cast another vote for myself.

I will learn from, rather than bury, a negative result.

Bottom line: I'm not burying the impact or lessons.

I lean in.

I lead through it.

For that I am grateful.

Deep

Why Do You Cry?

Little girl, why do you cry?
Because I do not understand
What is it that you do not understand?
Why it is better to die than to live
But that is not so, of course it is better to live than die.
Whatever gave you the idea it was not so.
Asked to kill, I took life
It was a frightening experience, but the worst part was
the ending, such stillness
Asked to give my own body and to touch, I gave freely
It too was frightening and at times painful, but there was not the
stillness, no, there
Was such life and energy.
Asked what I liked about my life, I said I like to touch
I offered to show others how
I was told I was evil
I decided it must be better to die than to live
Nobody spoke about the stillness, therefore it must have been okay

Young woman, why do you cry?
Because I have begun to understand
What is it you understand
Why it is better to live than to die
But then why do you cry?
Asked to touch, I have said no – I am evil
Asked to kill again, I have taken my own life

*It has been a frightening experience, the worst part being the
stillness at the end*
Today I learned something new
I think the tears are in honor of the little girl, she was not so dumb
*Nobody spoke of the stillness, because the stillness was all that
they had known*

Old crone, why do you cry?
Because I understand
What is it that you understand?
That life is both living and dying
But why do you cry?
Because it so painfully hard to see through one's own eyes
*The innocent child almost died but was saved by accepting the
life before her eyes*
*The young woman almost died by taking her own life because
she no longer was*
*Willing to look through her own eyes, but asked to see only as
others saw*
I, the old crone, live, seeing through the eyes of both
My tears are joy and sadness
*Joy, because the child's eyes did not close and the young woman
was willing to grow*
*Sadness because it was so hard and so slow and now it is
approaching the time I must go*

17.

Relational Not Right

"I was devastated when I heard Virginia Satir (a leader in humanistic psychology) say she wouldn't work with our family. She made it clear she had worked with Susan and heard someone in our family tell her *you'd be better off dead*. I just ..." My mom was shaken and teary.

"I'd reached out to Virginia, and I've no memory of anyone saying that to Susan. I do know things were very difficult." She shared through a choked voice.

What surprised me as I listened to my mom's words were *my* tears.

She continued to share what she'd felt and her struggle to make sense of it when the fabric of our family was ripped apart.

"I honestly did not know what to say to Susan when she asked me why I said *you'd be better off dead*. I didn't know how to answer. I have no memory of saying that. I don't think I was just trying to cover up."

Her voice was quaking.

I was trembling as well. I felt her angst. This was so very different from my own version of events. I was deeply moved.

Her reality was different from mine. It was not about who was right. The pain I felt was real. So was hers. Two stories. Different impacts. What I heard impacted my life.

Changed the trajectory. What she heard from Virginia Satir changed hers. Does it matter now who was right? NO.

Ben, one of our two facilitators, looked over to me and asked gently, "Susan, what's going on for you?"

I continued to let the tears roll down my cheek and said, "I am struck by how painful that must have been for her." I said through a trembling voice.

"I admit, I thought this was going to be about me finally getting to say my peace. It was going to be about *them* listening and confirming *my* reality. Maybe this is more important.

"I'm moved by your courage, Mom, to show up based on what you believe happened." I looked up at her. I felt empathy without agreement. Connection without one reality. I felt for this woman and the pain she had experienced as a mother.

I WANT TO LIVE

When I left Virginia in 1985 and moved to The Haven on Gabriola Island in British Columbia, Canada, I had no intention of looking back.

I had left with the words, "You'd be better off dead." ringing in my ears.

I also knew down in my bones that speaking my truth is what turned around my health. I no longer wanted to die.

I walked away and moved about as far away as possible.

I was angry.

I was hurt.

I didn't trust anyone really.

For almost 10 years that is the way it stayed prior to the above conversation.

TIME TO RECONNECT

In the final stages of completing my master's in family systems, I had been excused from doing the family interviews because of the traumatic process I had shared.

However, I'd been getting a nudge from inside that I did want to reconnect. I had been living on Gabriola Island and avoiding any contact with family.

I had put my life back in order and was feeling more consolidated with the fragmented story of my past.

What I appreciated about the leaders at The Haven is their approach to not wasting time to find "the truth" but instead helping me face and integrate "my truth" and deal with the emotional landscape created.

At the time I reached out to my family to reconnect, I'd completed my diploma in counseling at The Haven. I was leading Haven core programs.

I had spent an intensive month with Virginia Satir in her family systems program. I was finishing my master's and now in the third and final year of completing integrative body psychotherapy.

This nudge that kept coming was based on the belief that if I was going to do this work with other people, I needed to rebuild a bridge and connection with my own family.

I asked Ben, Jock, and Joann (the core leaders at that

time at The Haven) if they would do a family consult over a long weekend with my family.

"Yes, but we really think if your family comes — they are the courageous ones. We'll hold you to the highest level of staying present and engaged as the adult you can be," Jock said.

"I would want that." I wasn't certain I could stay present and I deeply appreciated their belief that I could.

Often over the years, I had been triggered or allowed my history to flood and override my staying in the present.

It wasn't like that reaction was gone, but I did have a lot more resources. I really valued those people who held me as able and provided me the feedback to relocate and connect.

Message received. They would facilitate without making it "safe" for me. They wanted to make it "safe" for my family to show up.

THE WEEKEND REUNION

Not all of my family came but each member shared personally and vulnerably about why they would come and why they would not.

One of my sisters was very clear. "You cut me off when you cut them off. I am not ready to reconnect yet."

Much earlier when I first got cancer, she'd shown up to a family therapy session that had been a disaster. She had said, "Something was definitely wrong with her growing up." Which had made me feel validated. However, it did not get handled well.

I had forgotten about that in my 10 years of distance and had missed milestones in her life. It sunk in how much pain she had felt due to my actions. In her mind, she hadn't done anything to deserve the way I treated her by cutting her out.

I appreciated her integrity and honesty in that statement. I really had not considered the impact on her in my cutoff. I felt that and it was an important piece for me to get.

This wasn't all about me!

It was a collection of adults coming together. Four of us (Mom, Dad, Penny, and myself) from the original family. Rob and Annmarie as partners to Penny and myself at the time.

We each had very different lives now, and frankly, very different lives even back then!

THE VALUE OF NO RIGHT OR WRONG

When I work with people now, I tell them, you always have to choose: Do you want to be right or relational?

This came home to me at the family reconnection.

I went in thinking I wanted some confirmation — *to be right.*

Though I think this is a bit sneaky because I didn't say I had to be right. I just said I didn't want to be all wrong. Just another form of having to be right.

In the end, that weekend made it very clear, *if I wanted a relationship with my family I needed to listen and be relational.*

I had to listen to their story and appreciate how it was for them. Those moments surprisingly were the moments that transformed my life.

Because having empathy and listening didn't take any-thing away from who I was. No. It simply made room for them. It made their experience real, and I could be relation-al. Without them needing to do anything for me.

That was incredibly empowering.

Ben Wong often said, "You don't need to be loved — you need to tap into your loving."

The family reunion brought that message home to be.

In listening and being able to understand their world and have empathy for them, I experienced my loving. I experi-enced the connection that comes from being a whole sepa-rate person and seeing another and how they put their world together.

I did deeply appreciate how it was for them.

I think they were loving. By showing up and coming to this island where they might be seen as monsters. They came. They shared. They sat and listened.

Yes, going in I did think they needed to confirm my story if they loved me.

That didn't matter. What mattered was I touched my loving without the confirmation that I was right or wrong, and I was free.

18.

The Sister Calls

"Mom's dementia is getting worse, we need to up her care," Melissa said with the commitment of one who had only recently lost her husband to pancreatic cancer.

"I'm not sure we can get Dr. J. to prescribe anything without taking her in for evaluation and we are totally shut down here." Penny, the oldest and the one with her hands directly on most things related to Mom.

Dare I say anything? Okay, what the hell. "Look, I'm not sure about more pills or evaluation. Mom is a people person, and she has no contact right now — none. We need to get a way to be in some contact and connection — what about GrandCare?"

"Okay, no electronics — no, no, no. I can't manage that!" Penny had the older sister dialed in — no extras, no electronics.

"Penny, we aren't there, and we know you are doing a lot. But we need contact. What is GrandCare?" Melissa had empathy, something I was missing in that moment.

"Why I thought of it was because you don't have to do anything. It is set up and even connects to medical." I honestly didn't know all the details yet but had started a process.

"I am not willing to go there. But maybe Clarke (my nephew) and you can talk — he thinks he can get her on Zoom." Penny had the final word.

Long sigh. I wasn't confident about Mom and Zoom, but I also knew my sister was NOT about to let go of too many of the threads she had holding her world around Mom and her family together.

TWO MONTHS LATER

"Mom, what is on your computer screen right now?"

"Zoom contacts." Her voice is tight, and I hear a click.

"Mom — please don't…"

"Now it's saying, 'Error message, do you want new upgrade?'"

Oh shit. Okay, stay cool.

What I know in this moment is that it is going to take a while to get her back on.

We get there.

"I see you — so good to have you visit." After 20 minutes of talking via the phone, I finally have her on Zoom for our "visit."

We have now had a few of these Zoom sessions — watched TED Talks and today's a puzzling session with Mom, myself, and Melissa.

We each have the same puzzle in Indiana, Montana, and Washington and have been doing short 10-minute puzzling sessions a couple times a week.

As we dive in — I hear a voice at Mom's door. "Bernie, I have your cookie and coffee."

"That is wonderful — can you please add cookies and coffee for my daughters." My mom calls back.

Both Melissa and I start talking "We aren't actually there ..." We say it together hoping to ensure that they don't think someone has snuck in.

Here's the deal.

My mom turned around when we started the Zoom connections.

Nothing was perfect about the situation.

But my mom didn't keep declining.

My sisters and I meet on Zoom each week.

Our calls were sometimes just about us and our worlds, also about Mom.

Let's go to that last call.

"I think we need to talk with Mom about what she wants." Penny was kicking off the call.

"Wants around what? Do you mean medical? Hearing aids or physical therapy? Visits or death and dying?!" I admit sometimes Penny's vague entry points bring out the worst in me. I was pretty sure my intensity was not helping the blunt death-and-dying piece land.

"Is Mom getting that much worse? How can we make sure she has the care she needs?" Melissa sounded panicked, and I thought I heard the tears I saw rolling down her face.

"Mom's physical therapist wants her to get her heart checked. She might need a pacemaker." Penny was now getting to the issues.

"A pacemaker — what the hell. I don't want her getting a pacemaker when her mind is going — what does she want?" Melissa was winding up. We had all gone through this with my dad. No extra medical care from his hospice bed turned into a pacemaker and two more years.

"That's why I want to have a conversation with Steve, a priest who was previously a doctor from my church." Penny, I could tell, already had a plan and now my heart was racing and an explosion was brewing.

"Wait — you've already..." No, *don't blow.* "We wanted a facilitated conversation with Mom about her desires while she can still do this right..." I was trying to hold back the internal swirl of my sister's desire to have that facilitator be a white man, a priest, and a medical doctor — that trifecta — was not a space I was in any way re-entering.

19.

The Three Sisters

The three sisters are plants (well, seeds) that individually are each important contributors to the table for a healthy, nutritious meal. The sisters are corn, beans, and squash. When these three seeds are planted together, the complementary ways in which they support, entwine, and collaborate is miraculous.

Indigenous people offered the wisdom of the three sisters. In the traditional story, the three seeds are planted together in one mound. In our garden, we have each variety of seed planted in very close proximity to each other.

The way the wisdom is translated through me is that the corn grows first — with purpose and rigidity towards the sky. The bean is the middle sister and joins later, first focused on leaves and spreading out, eventually weaving into the corn stalk, and using the stalk to find its way up. Once entwined with its elder sister, it grows very rapidly. The third sister takes the longest to sprout and moves out beneath the dirt away from the other sisters to develop and find nutrition. The leaves of the third sister are wide and low, covering and holding in the moisture, protecting the dirt and microbes from the sun for all three sisters. It is a beautiful, collaborative process.

As the third sister in my family, I can relate so much to the squash and can see my sisters as the corn and the bean.

So yes, this garden story has so much more for me than simple gardening wisdom.

I believe it also offers wisdom into what makes community, a family, and a team.

In my family, the three-sister application comes in our way of supporting my 93-year-old mother. My older sister, like the corn, is the person on the front line, doing the most direct work. I'd say a bit controlling but always there.

My middle sister provides the nitrogen needed. She provides the words of support and ensures that what happens on our calls isn't destructive. She's a translator and a connector. She also is amazing at providing that communication to both my mother and the team at her facility. I think of myself as the squash — a bit further out from the family yet still providing different connections for my mother in a time of isolation. Together it works.

Well, mostly.

These sister calls are as much a part of my life as the emerging stories.

Reconnecting with my family took years.

These days we have calls where the fractures and the cracks can happen quickly.

However, the warm and deep is ever present.

I wouldn't trade my family in for any other.

20.

Where Are The Ashes?!

There we were in the snake-like security line at SeaTac airport. When we had our IDs verified, my 90-year-old mother, in a wheelchair, was pushed by a TSA agent to a non-X-ray security line. I stood in my own TSA security screening line with my dad's ashes in The Ashes Bag, while holding a certified letter verifying the ashes.

As I got up to the TSA agent in my line, I handed her my letter. She then opened The Ashes Bag and pulled out my mother's pink nightgown. *What*?! I thought.

She dug deeper only to pull out a pair of granny panties. Looking at me with some concern and a bit of contempt in her eyes, she asked, "Where are the ashes?"

I stuttered, "Umm, they should be in there. I mean, they *were* in there." I reached to check inside the bag and the TSA officer quickly pulled it away. "Please don't touch your bag."

The TSA officer continued to pull various undergarments out of The Ashes Bag, as I turned all shades of red. *Where were the ashes that should be in The Ashes Bag?!* I was completely flustered.

"The ashes were in there last I checked."

How did I get into this situation, you may be wondering? I was wondering the same thing.

Why did I agree to travel to take my mom back to

Richmond, Virginia, to spread my dad's ashes? Virginia, and Richmond in particular, was a place I had experienced intense childhood trauma, and had some terror of returning to 30 years later.

MY FATHER'S INFLUENCE

In my opinion, it was always my dad's plan to get his way — even after he died. He tried to get us three sisters and Mom to go back to ol' Virginia. Sure, that sounds so innocent, right?

He couldn't get us to go back there when he was alive. So, he'd talked my sisters into agreeing to scatter his ashes in Virginia upon his death. He stipulated in his estate documents that he wanted his ashes scattered not in one, but in *seven different locations* in Virginia!

I'd sworn I'd never return to Virginia. There was more than one person who thought I'd be better off dead when I left based on some of the memories I brought up. So no, Virginia was not on my list to visit.

My two older sisters had a different experience. However, let's be clear: They both moved 3,000 miles across the country after college to the Pacific Northwest. I think there's something in that distance that speaks to the fractured family that grew up living most of our childhood at 3908 Rosedale Avenue in Richmond.

My dad is a bit of a paradox. He's the reason I love biking. He cycled until only a few weeks before he died in his nineties. However, biking with my father often involved getting lost and doing it his way. There were times in his later years when all we wanted was for him to stop riding that bicycle and try a tricycle because out there riding on his own, we never knew if he would make it back. I admired his grit but, boy, sometimes hated the stubbornness.

There were also the issues of the history that unfolded when I was ill. Up until his death, he would have moments where he'd pull me aside to say something about how it was someone else's fault, I started believing these crazy stories about my past. Just months before he died, I came to visit. He pulled me aside and asked if he was a good father. I told him that I thought he did the best he knew how and that I did not blame him.

His response: "I knew you would eventually tell me all those things never happened."

I felt so angry and in so many ways helpless. I did not want my father dying thinking I did not love him, but I was furious that once again my reality was being ripped out from under me.

All I could say was "If that is what you need to tell yourself to find peace — that is what I want for you."

I didn't hate him. There was much I loved about him. Paradox. Pain and joy. I still love riding back roads on my bike and I still try to tip my helmet to him when I find myself cycling a hill or mountain that most wouldn't dare to ride.

It is a common love between all three of us, my sisters and me. We each still love biking and we each do it in our own style. But always with a helmet and never with a map!

My father had lived all his life in the Richmond area, and

to his credit, had some very rich and wonderful connections.

However, this isn't a piece all about my father. But standing there in that TSA line with the ashes missing I couldn't help but wonder if my father wasn't still influencing the scene. He was not one for making a trip simple or a straight line.

BACK TO THE TSA LINE

As the TSA agent and I began to conclude The Ashes Bag contained only my mom's undergarments, my stress mounted. This was taking much longer than I'd planned. We were in jeopardy of missing our first flight. Still, no ashes found.

I had the ashes paperwork, but I surmised that my mom must have the ashes. My TSA agent took the letter and went over to my mom's line. Indeed, Bernadine did in fact have the ashes in her other bag.

We finally connected, and I returned the ashes to The Ashes bag, and we hurried to catch our first flight.

THE EVER-ELUSIVE ASHES

We did make it to Virginia. The ashes did as well.

Now you still may be wondering — but how did I get there?

When my sisters lined up the plans for my father's final trip home, they managed in their plans to create an impossible choice for my mother.

My cousin's son was getting married the weekend *after*

my father's memorial. My mom wanted to attend both the memorial and the wedding, but each of my sisters could only do one. Their individual travel plans left mom with a gap where she'd be alone in Virginia.

I stepped up and agreed to travel with her and fill the gap.

I'd bring her out to Virginia with the ashes and be there for the memorial and ashes scattering. I would stay with her in between the memorial and when my oldest sister arrived for the wedding.

As I was booking our travel, I admit I was very uncomfortable. My past, that was one thing, but traveling back home with my mom and my father's ashes — well, that seemed insane!

REVISITING MY CRAZY

We made our first flight because it was delayed. This seemed like a blessing, until the minutes ticked by, and we sat on the tarmac not moving.

"Oh my god, we're going to miss our next flight. We'll never make it. They'll leave without us." My mom was starting to get pretty upset about our situation.

Her concerns echoed my own. However, I had to admit looking at this mirror was quite sobering and uncomfortable. *Is this what I sound like when sitting next to CrisMarie on our trips?*

"We need to leave now. Why aren't we taking off? They're not telling us anything. Isn't someone going to do something?!" Bernie continued escalating.

"*Breathe and settle yourself*" was my internal mantra. Honestly, as she worried about connections and went on about how we weren't going to make it, I could not help but notice how my own reactions were so similar. I started to laugh.

It's not like you want to learn you are your mother's child because of shared neurotic tendencies. But you know when rugs get pulled out from under your reality about your biological father — I was glad to take anything that kept some sense of connection. Why not our shared travel neurosis?

Truth is that my mom and I shared some other interesting things. She, like me, is a horrible speller and probably dyslexic. She loved Healing Touch, an energy-based work that provided some common ground for us to relate. Not everyone in the family liked it — WOO! But my mom and I both had a strong belief and appreciation for the invisible forces of energy and spirit that I honestly think allowed for a thread of connection even in our most irreconcilable differences about the reality of my history and some things that never added up in any straight lines.

I took the neurotic similarities between me and my mom as a positive survival trait we shared. In this scenario, she had much more reason to be anxious. I needed to chill.

I did, though, share at some point up in the air what I was thinking about. To her credit she did giggle and smile, "I can get a bit wound up, can't I?"

That was a sweet moment in the midst of the chaos.

I did venture a step further and asked her about the moving of the ashes.

"I thought he'd prefer not to be labeled and so obvious,

I stashed the ashes in my suitcase. I wanted to keep him safe," she shared. This was not the response I was expecting, but had to smile. He, my father, would have liked that.

I did, though, insist that she not do that again. She agreed.

THE MEMORIAL

We arrived in Virginia and got settled in at the hotel. The next day was the memorial.

When we arrived at Hollywood Cemetery, it was a gray cloudy day. Let me just say this place was quite the outdoor museum, a living story in stone, iron, and landscape, and of course a place I could see why my father wanted to come back and rest here. It was rainy on and off, so settling my mom in under the tent with The Ashes Bag seemed to be important.

People started to arrive and there was much laughter and stories being shared. In many ways, it was a beautiful collection of the aspects of my father's life — from school connections to the many people part of various bicycling clubs, to people from church communities my parents had been connected to through the years. After some moving stories and at least one song it came time to scatter the ashes.

I kneeled and grabbed the bag next to my mom's seat and opened The Ashes Bag — all I found was another nightgown and dug around — no ashes.

What is it with Mom, nightgowns, and ashes?

"Mom, where are the ashes? I thought we agreed to keep them in The Ashes Bag." She was flustered and I wasn't really in a patient mood.

What was it about the ashes? This was the whole point of this trip. Where were the ashes?!

I went to tell my sister.

She said not to worry. She pulled out Dad's favorite old cookie tin. There she had "backup ashes." Thank goodness!

There are so many things I could write about here. The cookie tin — really? Okay, I sort of knew it had been part of the family from our years in Richmond. My father would stash candy or a cookie in it for months, maybe longer. Did my sister just come up with that brilliance or was this one of my father's odd but perfect ways of dealing with his ashes? If his treats and a cookie could live forever in that cookie tin — why couldn't he! He had always said he intended to somehow stick around, and these ashes proved that to be true.

I had to laugh.

The memorial service went off as planned.

THE PULL OF CRAZY

On the surface this trip was about my father and the ashes. However, there was so much more to it for me.

I felt the pull of my crazy. I had moments of terror and uncertainty. I went places that filled my dreams with nightmares. I slept through and woke up knowing that crazy still had some roots; however, it wasn't my homeland. I also had moments of laughter and joy at the crazy stories shared about my dad and with friends.

For a few nights my mom stayed with friends, while I stayed at the hotel. I went over to visit, and I listened to these friends' versions of what they believed had happened to me. Mostly quite different from the version I had. I made a couple of trips to the store that night to break up the tension for myself.

I knew this wasn't the time to get caught up in fighting for one reality.

I didn't need to fight or fear for myself. I listened for as long as I could, then took a break.

At some parts, I laughed, cried at a few others.

When I spoke, I mainly shared how I pulled the pieces of me back together to become who I am today.

Each night I was in Richmond I wondered if I was going to get through the vortex I swore I would never be in again.

But you know when you willingly walk into a storm, fire, or vortex — you get to choose how you walk through that storm — and I decided to walk through with my eyes and heart wide open.

TAKING THE ASHES

Melissa, her husband, and I took most of the ashes to the various locations. Indeed, it was a bit of a walk down a memory lane. Of course, our memories were different — but we shared and laughed, cried, and even agreed on the locations we weren't going to visit.

To honor my dad, we found people who wanted to take those ashes and made the deliveries.

All in all — between the moments with my mom and the moments with my sister — I found new memories and was able to keep my heart open.

I went back home. Yes, I went a little crazy, but I came out of it. I was able to scatter the ashes of my father amongst the trees and dirt of where my life went through hell and back — and I am better for that journey.

I'd like to believe it was my father's way of saying you aren't crazy. Ashes don't hold on to stories the same way our minds do! Taking the ashes back doesn't have to involve who's right and wrong, it's just a way of covering the shared terrain.

I could hold his ashes and even take them to places where I would never have chosen to return. Taking his ashes was a way of finally letting go of having to fight about who was right.

As I walked on through these places and listened to stories of my father, and my family, I had moments of wanting to fight or scream about how it just wasn't like that.

However, I listened and stayed quiet.

Much like before, I woke at night with some flashes and fears. However, I hugged my crazy and let the tears roll.

I'd get back up and take those ashes somewhere. Hear more stories. Laugh, cry, question, and breathe.

Ashes to ashes — dust to dust — we cycle through stories through our years and there is a time when we do need to let them go.

The ashes brought me closer to my mom.

The journey helped me know I could crack and not break.

A Phoenix Rising

Gathered in celebration
A celebration of acceptance and existence
The Phoenix rises
Up from the ashes
The light shines
Where there was always darkness
Illumination

One child, whose spirit did not die
Encapsulated by armor and defiance
Determined to survive and never hurt again
Touched by the soft, salty tears of a man
The strength of a circle
And the gentle music calling the spirit forth into the light

The dance began
The journey back home
Moments of terror
But the circle held
New faces filling any holes
An incredible circle
Dancing with the young woman
Through the anger and armor
Patiently waiting for her to find her own strength
As she spoke others joined in her screams
She was never alone
Friends in support, not in hate

Finding the path of light, not in revenge or justice
But in acknowledgement
Revelation
Acceptance

Today the circle joins again
In awe of the human spirit
The ability of the Phoenix to rise
Not in one but in us all

Together we are joined in the journey
Each rising from the depths of our own ashes
Choosing life
With its darkness
Its fire
And its incredible light
May the light of all of our efforts be an inspiration
This moment "privileged locus."

About The Author

Susan B. Clarke is a coach, consultant, and group facilitator. Since her own transformational health journey, she's focused her life on living fully in each moment and creating fulfilling relationships. Her passion comes in working with people to help them value differences, bring more of themselves to everything they do, and engage in the power of people working collectively together. With her partner, CrisMarie Campbell, she started Thrive! inc. Together they have written two books, *The Beauty of Conflict, Harnessing Your Teams Competitive Advantage* and *The Beauty of Conflict for Couples*. She lives in Whitefish, Montana and enjoys being out in nature, playing and learning from horses and her two dogs, Rosie and ZuZu.

Acknowledgements

A heartfelt shoutout to the many friends who have support-
ed this process.

Suzanne Muirhead, I love your art. Jackie ShannonHollis,
you are an inspiration and a wonderful writing mentor.
Robin Kelson, you are an amazing being and your love and
commitment to giving this book legs and wings did indeed
make it possible. CrisMarie, of course I cannot forget you!
Finally, to my sisters, I love you. Our stories are different
and even through the fractures and cracks, our desire to stay
connected has been stronger — love you both!

CPSIA information can be obtained
at www.ICGtesting.com
Printed in the USA
LVHW011947110122
708307LV00002B/203